Campgrounds of Los Angeles and Orange Counties

Federal, State, County, Regional, Municipal

14

5

LOS ANGELES
COUNTY

101

210

10

PACIFIC OCEAN

405

NORTH

ORANGE
COUNTY

0   10   20   30
MILES

Campgrounds of Los Angeles and Orange Counties

Federal, State, County, Regional, Municipal

Jeff Tyler

Sunbelt Guidebooks and Maps
"Natural Adventures in the Californias"
A series edited by Lowell Lindsay

SUNBELT PUBLICATIONS
San Diego, California

Sunbelt Publication, Inc.
P.O. Box 191126
San Diego, CA 92159-1126
(619) 258-4911 (619) 258-4916 fax
www.sunbeltpub.com

06 05 04 03 02   5 4 3 2 1

Library of Congress Cataloging—in—Publication Data

Tyler, Jeff (Jeff H.)
      Campgrounds of Los Angeles and Orange Counties: federal, state,
      county, regional, municipal/Jeff Tyler.—1st. ed.
           p.cm.—(Sunbelt guidebooks and maps)
      Includes bibliographical references and index.
      ISBN 0-932653-46-4
        1. Camp sites, facilities, etc.—California—Los Angeles County—
      Guidebooks. 2. Camp sites, facilities, etc.—California—Orange
      County—Guidebooks. 3. Los Angeles County (Calif.)—Guidebooks.
      4. Orange County (Calif.)— Guidebooks. I. Title.
      II. Series

CV191.42.C2 T92 2002
647.9794'9309'025—dc21

                                                            200105481

All photos by Jeff Tyler unless otherwise noted.

Contents

vi

Preface

I am always being asked, "At 15 million people and growing, where, if anywhere, in all this asphalt can there be public campgrounds in Los Angeles and Orange counties?" Answer: "They are here!" "And where is 'here'?" Well, as we did when I was a kid , you go to the beach, you go to the mountains, or you go to the desert. The area has all three. Whether it was better then depends on your point of view.

Most of L.A.'s public beaches in those days were for day use only. There was no camping, although Tin Can Beach in Orange County, unmanaged and unsupervised, did see many weekend tents. Standard for many of us older teenagers in those days was a weekend at the Tin Can, camping among the tents, cans, and bottles that made the place...unique. It was a strip of county beach a mile or so west of Huntington Beach and lying between the P.E. tracks (Pacific Electric, the interurban to you newcomers) and the ocean. It had no trash barrels, no toilets, nothing. It was said that the more macho aficionados brought sleeping bags, dug a shallow trench in what might be unencumbered sand, installed sleeping bag therein, and the retained heat in the sun-heated sand made for quite a comfortable night. Of course the sleeper had to be knowledgeable about tides, as a high tide could dispel the comfort.

We also used to camp in the San Gabriel Mountains, particularly in Big Tujunga Canyon, adapting to tents as the rocky soil discouraged trenching—as did the forest ranger. For the most part, when not at the beach, we older types made for the San Gabriels.

I was first introduced to the area when a buddy named Bill and I induced our parents to drop us off in Big Tujunga Canyon for a week. In a tent. On our own. It took some doing with tales of need in getting ready for upcoming Boy Scout tests and the enhancing of our outdoor skills. We even threw in that we would take some books along to study for school which would "soon be starting." Yes, yes. They finally relented, but I had the feeling they were not entirely fooled.

This was proven three days later when Bill's folks showed up to take us home. It was probably just as well. Cooking was a mystery, let alone over a camp fire. Our fresh food had succumbed to spoilage and insects. Eating was done cold and directly from the can. The sounds of the night were completely foreign and ominous. With all this, Bill, in a fit of pique, hiked off, on his own, the

11 miles down the canyon to a small gas station and phoned home. We were not quite as buddy-buddy for awhile after that. However, when school started, it was a different story. Paul Bunyan's biographer couldn't have told it better.

Today Tin Can Beach is gone. Part of it is now the excellent Bolsa Chica State Beach. Big Tujunga has changed, suffering from floods over the years. But the San Gabriels' vistas and streams are still there. In addition, there are many campgrounds that are well laid out, having fire rings, picnic tables, and other amenities we couldn't have dreamed of.

Campgrounds of Los Angeles and Orange Counties, like other books in this series for southern California, contains up-to-date, recently field-checked information on the county's public camps. Whether you're planning to camp in your RV or in a tent pulled from the trunk of your car, I have endeavored to provide all of the necessary information you'll need for your next camping experience.

The book is divided into two counties, with each county divided into two major sections: Coastal Campgrounds and Mountain Campgrounds. In addition, the Mountain Campground section is divided into five subsections, Hungry Valley/Pyramid Lake, Santa Clarita, Little Rock/Mount Gleason, Mount Wilson/Chilao/Crystal Lake, and Big Pines. Campgrounds have been assigned numbers that correspond to their locations on each area's map.

The descriptions contain information on the general settings and features of each campground: fees, number of sites, facilities, contact information, and directions for getting there. In addition, the appendix includes a directory of phone numbers and addresses, and sections on rules and regulations, Adventure Passes, and hazardous critters you might encounter while camping.

Campground conditions can change rapidly—storm and fire damage, budget constraints, and closings to protect sensitive habitats can all affect a campground. Campgrounds often fill up quickly during the summer months. When in doubt, contact the agency having jurisdiction over the campground before making the trip.

I've tried to provide accurate information. If you find, after visiting a campground, that I've overlooked important features, I welcome your comments via correspondence to the publisher .

Jeff Tyler
October 2001
Rio Bravo, California

Los Angeles County

Los Angeles County ranks twelfth in size among California's 58 counties (4069 square miles). It also is home to the City of Los Angeles, second largest in the United States. Yet within its borders are 47 public campgrounds and most settings are represented—seaside, mountains, desert, lakes. Many are near population centers, just as many offer secluded isolation. In all, the camper is afforded a wide range of choices, be it setting, degree of isolation, or activities of interest.

View from Highway 2

LOS ANGELES COUNTY COASTAL AREA

▲ 1. Leo Carrillo State Beach
▲ 2. Malibu Creek State Park
▲ 3. Topanga State Park
▲ 4. Dockweiler State Beach

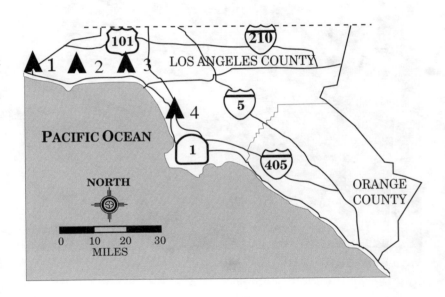

Leo Carrillo State Beach

GENERAL SETTING (LOCATION, FEATURES, SUPPLIES, INFORMATION) This 1600-acre state beach is located near the Ventura County line, between Malibu and Point Mugu. The campground is situated back in the hills, away from the beach, in the wide Arroyo Sequit Canyon. Eucalyptus trees, sycamore trees, and chaparral create a scene of rustic beauty and partly shade the sites. A campfire center with a stage, benches, and a fire ring is at the camp's north end. Hiking trails lead into the coastal hills.

South of the campground, there is access to the beach. Activities include surfing, windsurfing, beach walking, fishing, and observing tide pools. Swimmers are cautioned that lifeguards are on duty only during summer.

At times, nature walks are conducted by the ranger. The visitor center, open limited hours during summer, is located at the North Beach area. The small picnic area nearby has an ocean view.

Supplies and gasoline are available in Malibu. The state beach store, located at the campground in the canyon, carries limited supplies and is open during summer; phone for hours. For additional information, write or phone Leo Carrillo State Beach.

SITES, FEES, FACILITIES, TIME LIMITS The campground has 140 family campsites for tents or RVs (no hookups). The nightly fee is $12 per site. The camp road and parking spurs are blacktop. Campsites are dirt and with some grass. The maximum RV length is about 31 feet. A camp host resides at times in camp.

Each family site has a picnic table and a metal fire ring (with grill). Wheelchair-accessible restrooms have sinks, hot (pay) showers, flush toilets, and outdoor laundry tubs. The camp has water spigots, drinking fountains, an RV dump station ($3 for day-use), an RV water station, trash cans, dumpsters, and recycling bins. Pay phones, newspaper vending machines, a soft drink vending machine, and two picnic tables are located at the state beach store.

The primitive group site for tents (not RVs) is at the north end of camp near the campfire center. The nightly fee of $37 includes a maximum of 50 people and 16 vehicles. These vehicles must be parked in the parking lot that is next to the campfire center and is across the camp road from the group site. No camping is permitted in the parking lot. A restroom and pay phone are nearby. Anyone 17 years old or younger must have a parent's written consent.

Most campsites are reservable. Reservations are recommended, especially during summer.

The hike and bike area has five sites, each with a table and a fire ring. The nightly fee is $1 per person. A restroom is nearby.

In the parking lot for en route overflow camping, the fee is $12 per site, for one night only. Portable chemical toilets are available.

The picnic area has picnic tables, concrete barbecues, portable chemical toilets, trash cans, and a blacktop parking lot nearby. The day-use beach area near the underpass has restrooms and a blacktop parking lot. The day-use parking fee is $3 per vehicle.

Note: Heavy storms wiped out the North Beach area's 32 campsites; future plans for that area are indefinite, at the time of this writing.

Caution: The maximum height for all vehicles accessing the beach is 8 feet, because of the low-clearance underpass. At the underpass, the road to the beach is crossed by the creek and is flooded during storms. Dogs are not allowed on the beach.

Leo Carrillo State Beach's canyon camping area is usually open all year. From March to November, the camping limit at family sites is seven days. From December to February, the limit at family sites is 15 days. The limit at the group-site is seven days, year-round. The limit at en route overflow sites is one night, year-round.

DIRECTIONS From central Malibu, take State Highway 1 (Pacific Coast Highway) west about 15 miles to the Leo Carrillo State Beach access road (just before reaching Mulholland Highway). Turn right (north) and go a short way to the entrance.

Malibu Creek State Park

GENERAL SETTING (LOCATION, FEATURES, SUPPLIES, INFORMATION) This state park in the Santa Monica Mountains, north of Malibu, is not far from major arteries leading to Los Angeles, yet retains a country atmosphere. This is noticeable in the many backcountry trails for hiking, bicycling, and horseback riding which provide hours of quiet relaxation.

The state park occupies a small, coastal valley. High, rugged, chaparral-covered peaks along the western side of the park contrast with gently rolling, oak-spotted, grassy hills to the north.

The park's family camping area is nestled in its own little corner with some campsites set on the foot of a slope. Boulders dot the area, and some campsites are shaded by oaks.

The walk-in group campsite is set on a gentle incline at the southern edge of the valley, less than half a mile from the family camping area. The site is heavily shaded by oaks and has a nice view of a meadow and of the hills to north. A narrow hiking trail leads south, on which no dogs or bikes are allowed.

The park's picnic area is situated in a wide, open meadow surrounded by trees. Ramadas provide shade, and single-rail fences enhance the park's country atmosphere. A sizable trailhead parking lot is available for day use of the backcountry trails.

Malibu Creek State Park comprises more than 8000 acres, and now includes Tapia Park, a day-use picnic area that is 1.5 miles south of the state park entrance. Tapia Park's picnic sites sit on oak-shaded slopes rising from the road in Malibu Canyon.

The park's visitor center is open weekends and holidays. Supplies and gasoline are available in western Calabasas, about 3 miles north of the park, and in Malibu, about 6 miles south. For more information, write or phone Malibu Creek State Park.

SITES, FEES, FACILITIES, TIME LIMITS The family camping area has 63 numbered family campsites for tents or RVs (no hookups). The nightly fee is $12 per site. The camp road and parking spurs are blacktop; some spurs are not level. Campsites are dirt with some grass. The maximum RV length is about 30 feet.

Most family sites have a picnic table and a metal fire ring (with grill). The family camping area has water spigots, dumpsters, and information boards. Restrooms have sinks (indoors and outdoors), solar (pay) showers, flush toilets (some with wheelchair access), electrical outlets, and outdoor laundry tubs.

The group campsite is for tents (not RVs). The nightly fee is $45 and includes up to 60 people and 10 vehicles. These vehicles must be parked in the parking area, from which there is a short walk to the site.

The group campsite has picnic tables, large pedestal barbecues, a water spigot, a drinking fountain, and dumpsters. Restrooms have outdoor sinks, solar showers, flush toilets, and outdoor laundry tubs. The site's road, parking area, and grounds are dirt.

Reservations are recommended for all campsites. The RV water and dump station and a pay phone are located near the park entrance.

Malibu Creek State Park's picnic area has ramadas, picnic tables, pedestal barbecues, water spigots, restrooms, trash cans, dumpsters, and a gravel parking lot. A pay phone is located near the park entrance. The trailhead parking lot is blacktop and is situated near restrooms.

Tapia Park's picnic area has picnic tables, barbecues, restrooms, trash cans, and blacktop parking lots. The day-use parking fee at Malibu Creek State Park and Tapia Park is $2 per vehicle.

At Malibu Creek State Park (and Tapia Park), charcoal fires are permitted, but no wood fires. The campground is usually open all year. From May to November, the camping limit at family sites is seven days. From December to April, the limit at family sites is 15 days. The limit at the group site is seven days, year-round.

DIRECTIONS From central Malibu, take County Highway N-1 (Malibu Canyon Road) north about 6 miles to the park entrance road (just before reaching Mulholland Highway). Turn left (west). The dirt road to the group site is near the family camping area. It goes a quarter mile to the parking lot. Park and walk to the site.

Topanga State Park

GENERAL SETTING (LOCATION, FEATURES, SUPPLIES, INFORMATION) This huge state park of more than 10,000 acres, near Topanga in the Santa Monica Mountains, includes more than 35 miles of trails and fire roads for hiking, bicycling, and horseback riding. The nature center at the park entrance is open seasonally. Just beyond is the state park's parking lot and Trippet Ranch Trailhead at the bottom of the canyon, surrounded by dense woodlands of oaks. Nearby are a native plant garden and the old Trippet Ranch house, which serves as the park's headquarters.

Musch Trail Camp is the park's small, hike-in camp for hikers and equestrians. The camp is on Musch Trail, about a mile north of the parking lot; the trail is closed to vehicles. From the parking lot, a paved service road (gated to vehicles) leads north into a meadow. About a quarter mile farther, the narrow, dirt portion of Musch Trail forks to the east from the paved road. The trail drops down into a canyon with stream crossings, then winds its way up the canyon. In some places, many trees surround the trail with their branches arching over it, giving the effect of a jungle. While hiking to camp, see Saddle Peak and the rugged Santa Monica Mountains to the southwest, and the rolling chaparral hills to the east. Many spots command views of Topanga Canyon and its homes in the distance. More than half a mile after the trail veers east from the paved road, it ends at a gravel road. Walk to the right (east) and go about 500 feet to where Musch Trail continues to the north. The campground is a short distance farther. Look for the little white restroom building with its reddish brown roof.

The trail camp, situated in a small mountain meadow near the top of a hill, is partly shaded by eucalyptus trees and bounded by a split-rail fence. The camp's picnic tables are set along a narrow path by the fence, and a cactus patch is nearby. Beyond the fence, the terrain drops off to the north, down into a canyon. The camp has a view to the north of the hills and of another small meadow. The trail goes beyond camp, and reaches the Eagle Rock, a natural formation, after 1.5 miles.

Equestrian features at Musch Trail Camp include a hitching post and small corrals. Two small water troughs are available by the trail, west of camp. Horseback riding is allowed on Musch Trail.

Topanga State Park's two picnic areas are adjacent to the north and east sides of the parking lot. The north picnic area sits in an unshaded grassy clearing at the edge of a dense woodland. By contrast, the east picnic area is heavily shaded by tall oaks, and sits on a gentle canyon slope slightly below the parking lot.

Trippet Ranch Trailhead accesses several trails. Dead Horse Trail leads west to Dead Horse Parking Lot near Highway 27. The park's self-guided nature trail leads east; Sunday nature walks are conducted seasonally. Another trail leads southeast about 5 miles to Pacific Palisades and about 9 miles to Will Rogers State Park.

Supplies and gasoline are available on Highway 27 in Topanga, less than a mile south of Entrada Road. Supplies and gasoline are also available in Woodland Hills, about 8 miles north, and in Santa Monica. For further information, phone Topanga State Park.

SITES, FEES, FACILITIES, TIME LIMITS Musch Trail Camp accommodates 20 people, and the nightly fee is $1 per person (no reservations). At camp, eight horses are allowed, but no vehicles; vehicles must be parked in the parking lot near the park entrance.

The camp has eight picnic tables, two flush toilets, two outdoor wash basins, and a trash can (equestrian features: see above).

Topanga State Park's two picnic areas have picnic tables and trash cans. The north picnic area also has pedestal barbecues. A restroom with wheelchair-accessible flush toilets is located between the picnic areas. Drinking fountains are at this restroom and at the east picnic area. Information boards are provided. The park's parking lot is blacktop. The day-use parking fee is $2 per vehicle.

Note: Portable camp stoves are allowed at the trail camp, but no wood or charcoal fires are permitted. No pets are allowed.

Caution: Musch Trail is very narrow like a footpath. In some places, it is steep, winding, and crossed by streams or runoffs.

Musch Trail Camp in Topanga State Park is closed during periods of fire danger or heavy rains, but is usually open otherwise. The camping limit is seven days.

DIRECTIONS From central Santa Monica, take State Highway 1 (Pacific Coast Highway) northwest about 6 miles, and at State Highway 27 (Topanga Canyon Boulevard), turn right (north). Go 4.7 miles to Entrada Road, north of the town of Topanga. Turn right (east) and pass Dead Horse Parking Lot. Follow the signs that lead to Topanga State Park. Go about half a mile to a fork, and bear left, still on Entrada Road. Go about a quarter mile to another fork, bear left, and proceed to the park entrance and the parking lot. Hike north on Musch Trail about a mile to camp.

Dockweiler State Beach

GENERAL SETTING (LOCATION, FEATURES, SUPPLIES, INFORMATION) This state beach, located west of El Segundo, has a wide view of the Santa Monica Bay. The Palos Verdes Peninsula, at the southwestern end of the bay, and Point Dume near Malibu, at the northwestern end, can be seen when the fog lifts.

From the coastal road, the access road slants down the side of a bluff to the campground, which is level with the beach. Campsites are well spaced. Outer sites are more spacious and have views of the beach. Although the campground has no trees for shade, the ocean climate is usually pleasant throughout the year.

A paved bicycle pathway runs along the beach for more than 20 miles, and is used for bicycling, roller-skating, and strolling. Swimming, surfing, and surf fishing are other popular activities. *Caution:* Lifeguard service is provided only during summer.

The state beach lies barely a mile west of the Los Angeles International Airport runways from which jumbo jets continually take off, just before flying over the beach. People who don't mind aircraft noise will enjoy camping here. Aviation buffs can identify the various aircraft that fly overhead.

The Hyperion Sewage Treatment Plant is also nearby. If Dockweiler State Beach is not one of the most glamorous camping locations, it is definitely one of the most convenient. It is about halfway between the northern and southern ends of Santa Monica Bay, and is easily accessible to the bay area's sights and attractions.

Playa del Rey, Marina del Rey, Fisherman's Village, and Venice Beach are among the many attractions in the bay area to the north, reached by Vista del Mar (the coastal road) and State Highway 1. King Harbor at Redondo Beach is about 6 miles south, by way of Vista del Mar (the coastal road).

Supplies and gasoline are available nearby in El Segundo and in Manhattan Beach, a few miles south. Dockweiler State Beach is owned by the State of California, but is operated by the Los Angeles County Department of Beaches and Harbors. For more camping information, including group rates, phone the state beach's campground, Dockweiler RV Park.

SITES, FEES, FACILITIES, TIME LIMITS The camp has 83 full-hookup campsites for RVs. During summer, the nightly fee per site is $25; during winter, it is $22 for a beach row site or $17 for a second row site. The camp also has 34 non-hookup campsites for RVs. During summer, the nightly fee per site is $15; during winter, it is $12. No tents are allowed. For each vehicle, the city parking tax is $1.35 during summer, and $1 during winter. Campsites are reservable. The entire campground is blacktop. The maximum RV length is about 37 feet. Four wheelchair-accessible campsites are situated near the restrooms.

Each site has a picnic table and a pedestal barbecue. The camp has soft drink and water vending machines, a coin laundry, an RV dump station, trash cans, an information board, and restrooms with sinks, hot showers, and wheelchair-accessible flush toilets.

Dogs are not allowed on the beach; the nightly fee is $1 per dog. Near camp, the state beach has blacktop parking lots for day use. The day-use parking fee is $5 per vehicle, or $12 if the vehicle is large. The day-use fee to access the RV dump station is $5.

Check-in time is 1 P.M. and check-out time is 12 noon. The campground is usually open all year. The camping limit is 14 days.

DIRECTIONS From central Santa Monica, take I-10 east about 3 miles to I-405 in the West Los Angeles area, then go south about 8 miles to I-105 in Hawthorne. Go west on I-105, and after 1.5 miles, the freeway ends and merges into Imperial Highway in El Segundo. Continue west on Imperial Highway about 2 miles to the end of the highway and the state beach entrance at the coast.

LOS ANGELES COUNTY MOUNTAIN AREA

1. Hungry Valley Area
2. Santa Clarita Valley Area
3. Littlerock Area
4. Mount Wilson, Chilao Area
5. Big Pines Area

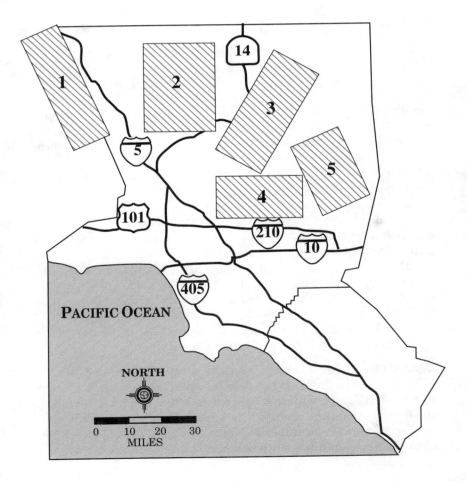

LOS ANGELES COUNTY MOUNTAIN AREA

HUNGRY VALLEY AREA AND PYRAMID LAKE AREA

■ Tejon Pass Rest Area

▲ 1. Hungry Valley State Vehicular Recreation Area (SVRA)

▲ 2. Los Alamos Campground

▲ 3. Oak Flat Campground

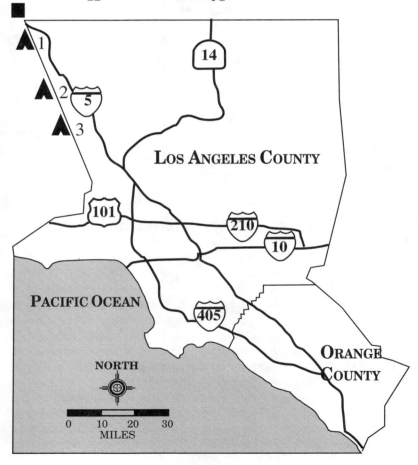

Tejon Pass Rest Area

Sycamore trees and lawns make this Caltrans rest area a pleasant place to stop and stretch, nearly midway between Valencia and Bakersfield (no camping allowed). It sits on both sides of I-5 in a wide canyon near Frazier Park in Kern County, just north of the Los Angeles County line. Fast-food restaurants and service stations are located nearby at Frazier Park, and in Gorman, just 3.5 miles south. *Tejon* is the Spanish word for *badger*, a local woodland critter. Fort Tejon State Historic Park is located about 4 miles north.

The rest area's RV water station and dump station serve several mountain campgrounds in the three-county border area (Los Angeles, Ventura, and Kern Counties). Other facilities include picnic tables, ramadas, drinking fountains, benches, pay phones, and information boards. Vending machines dispense newspapers, soft drinks, and snack foods. Restrooms have sinks and flush toilets and are wheelchair accessible, as are the rest area's paved pathways. Trash cans, recycling bins, and a pet area are provided.

From Valencia, take I-5 north about 36 miles. The rest area is just north of the Frazier Park exit, and south of the Lebec exit. State Highway 138, which leads east to Lancaster, Palmdale, and the Mojave Desert, is about 6 miles south of Tejon Pass Rest Area.

Hungry Valley State Vehicular Recreation Area (SVRA)

GENERAL SETTING (LOCATION, FEATURES, SUPPLIES, INFORMATION) This 19,000-acre SVRA is located south of Gorman. Registered vehicles such as motorcycles, four-wheel-drive vehicles, all-terrain vehicles (ATVs), and other off-highway vehicles (OHVs) can be driven on more than 100 miles of OHV trails. During spring, wildflower tours are given; phone for details.

Special OHV features, on the west side of the SVRA, include a mini-track for beginning riders at Smith Forks Campground, and a series of four-wheel-drive practice courses at Aliklik Campground. A fenced OHV loading dock with ramp is available at Edison, Smith Forks, Aliklik, and Lane Ranch Campgrounds.

On the east side of the SVRA, the Motocross Track, in the Quail Canyon Off-Road Event Area, is designed for use in competitive OHV events by organized groups and race promoters only, and is reservable (phone the SVRA). The primitive group camping area nearby may only be used for these special OHV events.

The SVRA entrance is on Gold Hill Road at Peace Valley Road, on the SVRA's north side, near Gorman. A quarter mile south of this entrance, on Gold Hill Road, there is a registration and information booth, a day-use parking area, a pay phone, a vault toilet, and a dumpster.

Supplies and gasoline are available nearby in Gorman, in Frazier Park, a few miles north, and in Valencia. For additional information, including road conditions and OHV regulations, write or phone Hungry Valley State Vehicular Recreation Area.

SITES, FEES, FACILITIES, TIME LIMITS There are nine primitive camps located on the west side of the SVRA, and most of them lie within Ventura County, which is not covered in detail in this book. The camps have a combined total of more than 140 non-reservable campsites for tents or RVs (no hookups).

Lane Ranch Campground is the only one of the nine camps that lies within Los Angeles County, and is blessed with the most shade trees. The camp is set in an open plain, away from the hills.

In the following list, each campground is followed by its total number of campsites: Edison 12, Sterling Canyon 12, Circle Canyon 20, Cottonwood 14, Upper Scrub Oaks 16, Lower Scrub Oaks 8, Smith Forks 20, Aliklik 15, and Lane Ranch 25. Upper Scrub Oaks Camp and Lane Ranch Camp each have a campsite that is wheelchair accessible.

The nightly fee is $6 per vehicle. The day-use fee is $4 per vehicle. Each camp's roads, grounds, and campsites are dirt with no grass. There are no parking spurs; parking is on the sites. Many sites can accommodate large RVs.

Each campsite has a picnic table, a metal fire ring (with grill), and a ramada, since the camps have few or no trees. Each ramada has its campsite number on it. All camps have vault toilets (most with wheelchair access), trash cans, and one or more dumpsters.

The SVRA has no piped water or RV dump stations. An RV water station and dump station are provided at Tejon Pass Rest Area, on I-5, north of Frazier Park, a few miles north of the SVRA.

Hungry Valley SVRA's campgrounds are usually open all year. The camping limit is 14 days. *Caution:* Roads in Hungry Valley are crossed in several places by streams and creeks. Heavy rains result in flooding. Gold Hill Road and Hungry Valley Road are mostly paved but have some potholes and short stretches of dirt.

DIRECTIONS From Valencia, take I-5 north about 33 miles to the Gorman exit in Gorman. Exit, turn left, and at Peace Valley

Road, turn right (northwest). Go about a mile to the Hungry Valley SVRA entrance at Gold Hill Road (Forest Road 8N01). The sign mentions Hungry Valley SVRA but not Gold Hill Road. Turn left (south) and enter the SVRA. The campgrounds are located along or near Gold Hill Road and Hungry Valley Road (5 miles south), at intervals of a mile or less.

Los Alamos Campground

GENERAL SETTING (LOCATION, FEATURES, SUPPLIES, INFORMATION) Pyramid Lake, a popular recreation spot, is just a few miles southeast of this large campground, located between Castaic and Gorman. The campground and Pyramid Lake are national forest units run by the same concessionaire. Camping is permitted at the campground but not at Pyramid Lake, which is a day-use area. The elevation at camp is 2600 feet.

The campground is spread over a low rise at the edge of the foothills, with a view of the valley. The view of the I-5 freeway in the distance, to the east, is a reminder that civilization is not so far away, after all. The campground includes a main camp with family campsites, and a group camp, half a mile west of the main camp. Family campsites are divided among three loops situated in short box canyons that reach into the foothills.

Pyramid Lake offers waterskiing, jetskiing, rental boating, and fishing for bass, catfish, and bluegill. Swimming (fee required) is allowed only at the swimming beach, which is open during summer and has lifeguard service. There are several picnic areas; some are near parking lots and have wheelchair access; others across the lake have docks and can be reached only by boat.

Pyramid Lake's marina features a snack bar, a general store with bait and tackle, boat rentals, a dock, and a boat launch ramp.

Vista del Lago Visitor Center is on Vista del Lago Road by I-5, about 3 miles south of Smokey Bear Road.

Supplies and gasoline are available near I-5 in Gorman, about 6 miles north of Smokey Bear Road, and in Valencia. The camp store, at the main camp's entrance, has limited supplies.

For campground information and Pyramid Lake boating regulations, phone the concessionaire or contact the Santa Clara/Mojave Rivers Ranger District Office of the Angeles National Forest.

SITES, FEES, FACILITIES, TIME LIMITS The main camp has 93 nonreservable, numbered family campsites for tents or RVs (no hookups). The nightly fee is $10 per site. The main camp has three loops with blacktop roads, gravel parking spurs, and dirt campsites. The maximum RV length is about 26 feet. Some sites have a tree and limited shade. Some campsites are paved and are wheelchair accessible. Restrooms are also wheelchair accessible.

Each family site has a picnic table and a metal fire ring (with grill). The three loops have water spigots, restrooms with sinks and pedal-flush toilets, and trash dumpsters, but no hookups.

The group camp accommodates 75 people. Three group campsites, identified by the letters A, B, and C, are for tents or RVs. The fee is $50 per group site, per night. Group reservations are required (phone the concessionaire for information). The three sites are dirt and are unshaded, although trees surround sites B and C. Each group site and the restroom has a small blacktop parking lot. The access road in the group camp is blacktop.

Each group campsite has a few picnic tables, a water spigot, a concrete fire ring (without grill), and a pedestal barbecue or a metal fire ring (with grill). The restroom has sinks, pedal-flush toilets, an outdoor laundry tub, and a dumpster.

For registered campers, an RV dump station is provided near the camp office. A pay phone is available at the camp office.

Pyramid Lake's picnic areas have picnic tables, grills, ramadas, wheelchair-accessible restrooms, and blacktop parking lots. The day-use parking fee is $6 per single vehicle, and $12 per vehicle with trailer.

The main camp's Loop 2 and the group camp are usually open all year. The main camp's Loops 1 and 3 are open from Memorial Day weekend to Labor Day weekend. The camping limit is 14 days.

DIRECTIONS From Valencia, take I-5 north about 26 miles to Smokey Bear Road. Exit, turn left (west), and go to Pyramid Lake Road. Turn left (south), and go 1.5 miles to Emigrant Landing. At Forest Road 7N32 (sign missing at this writing), turn right (west). Drive over the bridge and go about 2 miles to the main camp's entrance, then about half a mile farther to the group camp's entrance. Both entrances are located on the road's left (south) side.

To reach Pyramid Lake, do not turn at Emigrant Landing, but continue south on Pyramid Lake Road to the entrance.

Oak Flat Campground

GENERAL SETTING (LOCATION, FEATURES, SUPPLIES, INFORMATION) Oak trees are so common on the brown hills of California, that they often find their way into the names of roads, towns, and other places, including this flat and the camp that sits on it. Campsites are set in thick groves of oaks that provide ample shade during the hot summers. These particular oaks lose their leaves during autumn, and temporarily create a stark landscape of skeletons. The elevation at camp is 2800 feet.

This Angeles National Forest campground is conveniently located about halfway between two popular recreation spots, Castaic Lake and Pyramid Lake. Oak Flat Forest Station (not always in use) and Oak Flat Spring are near camp. Oak Flat and the campground sit above the highway on a low plateau lined with hills along its west side. Short log posts separate campsites.

A trailhead for the Piru Creek area is located where Golden State Highway ends, about 2 miles north of camp. This is a day-use area with a hiking trail that leads to Piru Creek, where fishing is permitted. A blacktop parking lot is provided at the trailhead. Frenchmans Flat, just west of the highway, is the location of a an old campground, long gone.

Supplies and gasoline are available in Valencia and Castaic. For more information, write or phone the Santa Clara/Mojave Rivers Ranger District Office of the Angeles National Forest.

SITES, FEES, FACILITIES, TIME LIMITS The campground has 27 nonreservable, numbered campsites for tents or RVs (no hookups). A parked vehicle requires an Adventure Pass. The camp's loop road, parking spurs, and campsites are dirt. The maximum RV length is about 18 feet.

Each campsite has a picnic table and a pedestal barbecue. Some sites also have a metal fire ring (with grill). The camp has vault toilets and trash cans, but no water. An RV water and dump station is located at Tejon Pass Rest Area, on I-5, north of Frazier Park (about 22 miles north of Templin Highway).

Oak Flat Campground is usually open all year. The camping limit is 14 days. *Caution:* The camp road is muddy during rains.

DIRECTIONS From Valencia, take I-5 north about 13 miles to Templin Highway. Exit, turn left (west), and at Golden State Highway, turn right (north). Go about 3 miles to the paved access road that leads to Oak Flat Forest Station and the campground. Turn left (west) and go about a quarter mile. Just beyond the forest station, turn right (north) at unpaved Forest Road 6N23, and enter the campground.

LOS ANGELES COUNTY MOUNTAIN AREA

SANTA CLARITA VALLEY AREA

▲ 1. Castaic Lake State
Recreation Area
▲ 2. Upper Shake Camp
▲ 3. Sawmill Camp
▲ 4. Bear Camp
▲ 5. Cienaga Camp

▲ 6. Cottonwood Camp
▲ 7. Zuni Camp
▲ 8. Streamside Camp
▲ 9. Spunky Camp
▲ 10. Walker Ranch Group Camp

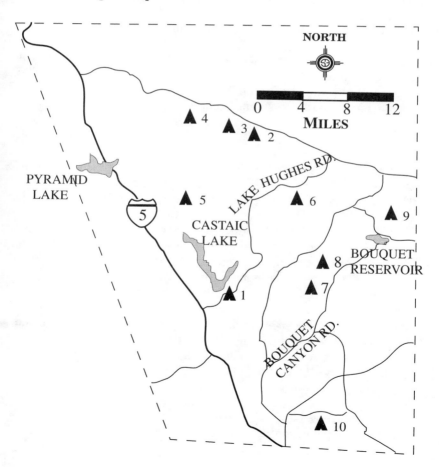

Castaic Lake State Recreation Area

GENERAL SETTING (LOCATION, FEATURES, SUPPLIES, INFORMATION) This 2035-acre aquatic recreation area is located around Castaic Lake (a reservoir) and Castaic Lagoon in the hills north of the Santa Clarita Valley. It is operated for the state by Los Angeles County Department of Parks and Recreation.

The fun includes waterskiing, jetskiing, windsurfing, boating, and fishing for trout (seasonally), bass, catfish, and bluegill. Boat rentals, boat launch ramps (fee), a fishing pier, and fishing supplies are available. Also featured are picnic areas on both sides of the lagoon, playgrounds on the west side, and trails for hiking, bicycling, and horseback riding. Portions of the recreation area are shaded by eucalyptus, cottonwood, and transplanted pine trees.

The recreation area's family campground, situated on Castaic Lagoon's eastern shore, includes three areas that have views of the lagoon and of the homes to the west, across the lagoon. The camp sits at the foot of steep low hills to the east. Areas A and B are developed with grass and some trees; Area A has more trees shading sites than B. Area C is primitive and unshaded, with bushes separating sites, and has a view of the dam nearby to the north.

The recreation area's group camp sits above the western shore on a grassy flat atop a hill from which there are partial views of the lake and lagoon to the east. The group sites, Seven Acres and Three Acres, are partly shaded by eucalyptus trees. Three Acres is the smaller site, with fewer facilities. Castaic Trail is for hiking, bicycling, and horseback riding. It connects the two group sites and goes along edge of the sites, overlooking the lagoon and lake.

Swimming is permitted seasonally, only in designated areas on the west side of the lagoon, and only when a lifeguard is on duty. Swimming is not permitted in the reservoir.

Magic Mountain amusement park in Valencia and Vasquez Rocks County Park in Agua Dulce are among the valley's varied attractions. The natural, jagged formations of Vasquez Rocks have been used in movies and television shows. Northwest of the rocks is the U.S. Forest Service's Rowher Flat OHV Area, which is off Sierra Highway, a few miles west of Agua Dulce Road.

The recreation area has a snack bar. Supplies and gasoline are available in Castaic. For reservations, aquatic regulations, and other information, contact Castaic Lake State Recreation Area.

SITES, FEES, FACILITIES, TIME LIMITS The family camp has 60 reservable, numbered family campsites for tents or RVs (no hookups). The nightly fee is $12 per site. Area A has 16 sites, B has 20 sites, and C has 24 sites. Areas A and B have blacktop roads and blacktop parking lots with parking spaces adjacent to dirt-and-grass campsites. Area C has a dirt road and dirt parking spaces and sites. The maximum RV length is about 35 feet.

Each family campsite has a picnic table and a metal fire ring (with grill). The camp has restrooms with sinks and flush toilets (some with wheelchair access), an RV water station, an RV dump station with a day-use fee of $3, and trash cans.

For group camping fees and reservations, phone the recreation area. The two group campsites have picnic tables, pedestal barbecues, drinking fountains, restrooms, trash cans, blacktop roads and parking lots, and dirt-and-grass sites. Seven Acres has ramadas, and Three Acres has a concrete fire ring (without grill).

Day-use picnic areas have picnic tables, pedestal barbecues or metal fire rings (with grills), some ramadas, drinking fountains, restrooms, and blacktop parking lots nearby. The day-use parking fee is $10 for each RV and $6 for any other vehicle.

Pay phones are available at the day-use restroom near the east entrance, which is near the family camp, at the park office near the main (west) entrance, and at the snack bar.

No dogs or other pets are allowed in the lagoon or lake. Check-in time is 2 P.M. and check-out time is 10 A.M. The campground is usually open all year. The camping limit is 14 days.

DIRECTIONS From I-5 in Castaic, take Lake Hughes Road east about half a mile to Ridge Route Road. Turn left (north) and go about half a mile to the recreation area's main (west) entrance. Turn right (east), go beyond the entrance station, and turn left (north). Go about a mile to the group sites. To reach the family camp, stay on Lake Hughes Road, and go about half a mile east from Ridge Route Road to the east entrance. Turn left (north) and proceed to the family camp.

Upper Shake Campground

GENERAL SETTING (LOCATION, FEATURES, SUPPLIES, INFORMATION) Although this campground is primitive and plunked in the middle of a somewhat rugged woodland setting, the scenery is attractive. The elevation of this Angeles National Forest camp, located west of Lake Hughes, is 4400 feet. The camp's access road drops down from the main forest road into a small canyon that is thick with chaparral, oaks, pines, firs, and riparian trees. As the access road approaches the camp, the canyon widens, and the camp sits on a little inclined shelf on the side of a hill above the stream. The road loops through the camp above the canyon bottom, and campsites sit on gently inclined slopes. The campground is well shaded.

A dirt parking area for the Pacific Crest Trail, a national scenic trail, is on Forest Road 7N23, about a mile west of the camp's access road. Lower Shake Camp, a little tent camp that was a few miles from Upper Shake Camp, has been removed.

For more about the area, see Sawmill Campground. Supplies and gasoline are available in Castaic, roughly 25 miles southwest of Lake Hughes. Limited supplies are available at Lake Hughes. For more information, write or phone the Santa Clara/Mojave Rivers Ranger District Office of the Angeles National Forest.

SITES, FEES, FACILITIES, TIME LIMITS There are 13 nonreservable sites for tents or RVs (no hookups). A parked vehicle requires an Adventure Pass. The road to camp is dirt. Parking spurs and the road in camp are old blacktop with some gravel. Sites are dirt with some grass. The maximum RV length is about 20 feet.

Each campsite has a picnic table and a metal fire ring (with grill). The camp has vault toilets, a trash bin, and information boards, but no water or hookups. RV water and dump stations are available at Tejon Pass Rest Area, on I-5, north of Frazier Park.

Upper Shake Campground is usually open from May to November. The camping limit is 14 days. *Caution:* The dirt roads leading to camp are narrow and winding with some rocky stretches and a few dips. The side road to camp has stream crossings. Large trailers and motorhomes are not recommended.

DIRECTIONS From Lake Hughes, take Pine Canyon Road (County Highway N-2) west about 5 miles to unpaved Forest Road 7N23. Turn left (south) and go 2 miles. Pass a gated road, then reach Forest Road 7N23B. Turn left (east) and go 0.7 mile to the campground at the end of the road.

Sawmill and Bear Campgrounds

GENERAL SETTING (LOCATION, FEATURES, SUPPLIES, INFORMATION) Impressive, sweeping views of the Antelope Valley are afforded to the north from Forest Road 7N23, which winds along or just below the ridges of Sawmill Mountain, where Sawmill Campground is located, and Liebre Mountain, where Bear Campground is located. The two ridges are connected by a saddle and are located between Lake Hughes and Gorman. To the south, chaparral hills can be seen, including Burnt Peak, with its microwave relay towers, and the Santa Clarita Valley in the far distance. The road rises higher toward more remote Bear Camp. These Angeles National Forest camps are small and primitive. The elevation is 5200 feet at Sawmill Camp and 5400 feet at Bear Camp.

Sawmill Campground sits on a rolling flat on the side of a hill, and is accessed by a road that drops down from the main forest road. Oaks and pines shade much of the camp. Some sites have partial views through the trees of the Antelope Valley below.

Bear Campground is nestled in a cozy little bowl-shaped depression on the ridge. Campsites sit on the gently sloping sides of the bowl and are partly shaded by oaks.

The Pacific Crest Trail parallels and crisscrosses Forest Road 7N23 between Burnt Peak Trailhead and Bear Camp. Burnt Peak Trailhead and a dirt parking area are located on Forest Road 7N23, 1.3 miles east of Sawmill Camp's access road. This trailhead accesses a gated road for hiking (not vehicles), that leads south about 3 miles to Burnt Peak (elevation: 5800 feet), and accesses unpaved Forest Road 7N08, which leads east about 10 miles to Lake Hughes. Another dirt parking area for the Pacific Crest Trail is on Forest Road 7N23, 1.4 miles west of Sawmill Camp's access road.

Atmore Meadows, a few miles southwest of Sawmill Camp, is a nice area for a hike. From the undeveloped trailhead at the end of Forest Road 7N19 in Atmore Meadows, two hiking trails lead several miles south to the Redrock Mountain area (not to be confused with Red Rock Canyon). Atmore Meadows Camp, a little tent camp near the end of the road, has been removed. Forest Road 7N19 to Atmore Meadows meets Forest Road 7N23 about 2 miles west of Sawmill Camp's access road. The crossroad sits in a saddle between Sawmill Mountain and Liebre Mountain. The Pacific Crest Trail meets Forest Road 7N19 just south of Forest Road 7N23.

Supplies and gasoline are available in Castaic, roughly 25 miles southwest of Lake Hughes. Limited supplies are available at Lake Hughes. For more information, contact the Santa Clara/Mojave Rivers Ranger District Office of the Angeles National Forest.

SITES, FEES, FACILITIES, TIME LIMITS Sawmill Campground has eight campsites for tents or small RVs (no hookups).

Bear Campground has six campsites for tents. All sites are nonre-servable. A parked vehicle requires an Adventure Pass. Both camps have dirt loop roads. Campsites are dirt with some grass. There are no parking spurs. Parking is on the sites at Sawmill Camp. At Bear Camp, park near the sites and walk to them. The maximum RV length is about 16 feet at Sawmill Camp.

At both campgrounds, each campsite has a picnic table and a metal fire ring (with or without grill). Each camp has a vault toilet and an information board, but no water or hookups. RV water and dump stations are available at Tejon Pass Rest Area, on I-5, north of Frazier Park. Carry out your trash.

Sawmill and Bear Campgrounds are usually open from May to November. The camping limit is 14 days. *Caution:* The dirt roads leading to the camps are narrow, winding, rocky in places, and have a few dips. Large trailers and motorhomes are not recommended. Sawmill Camp's access road is somewhat steep.

DIRECTIONS From Lake Hughes, take Pine Canyon Road (County Highway N-2) west about 5 miles to unpaved Forest Road 7N23. Turn left (south) and go 3 miles to Burnt Peak Trailhead and Pacific Crest Trail access. On Forest Road 7N23 (now heading west), go 1.3 miles to Forest Road 7N23A. Turn right (north) and go a quarter mile to Sawmill Camp. On Forest Road 7N23, go west 1.4 miles to another trailhead of the Pacific Crest Trail, then half a mile to Forest Road 7N19, which leads south about 2 miles to Atmore Meadows. On Forest Road 7N23, go west 3 miles to Forest Road 7N23E. Turn left (south) and go a short way to Bear Camp.

Cienaga Campground

GENERAL SETTING (LOCATION, FEATURES, SUPPLIES, INFORMATION) Though primitive, this national forest camp is situated in a quiet, appealing little valley, northeast of Castaic. The valley is also a wide place in a canyon of chaparral hills dotted by yuccas. The canyon walls are steep in places, and the U.S. Forest Service tower on the ridge above to the west is visible from some points along the dirt road leading to the campground.

Campsites are set along a loop road and are nicely spaced, with plenty room between. Some sites are shaded by sycamores, oaks, or cottonwoods, while other sites are out in the open. This camp seems more suitable for rugged individuals, and less suitable for families than Cottonwood Camp on Lake Hughes Road.

Cienaga Campground is located near Cienaga Spring, and a stream flows by camp. *Cienaga* means *marsh* or *swamp*, in Spanish. The elevation is 2100 feet. Near camp, a hiking trail leads north several miles to the Redrock Mountain area. About 4 miles east of camp, Forest Road 7N13 leads northeast a few miles toward Sawtooth Mountain, and Forest Road 7N132 leads south a few miles up Warm Springs Mountain to the summit with a view.

Warm Springs Campground, near Warm Springs Rehabilitation Center, has been removed. Supplies and gasoline are available in Castaic. Limited supplies are available at Lake Hughes, about 10 miles northeast of Forest Road 6N32. For more information, write or phone the Santa Clara/Mojave Rivers Ranger District Office of the Angeles National Forest.

SITES, FEES, FACILITIES, TIME LIMITS The camp has 14 nonreservable, numbered campsites for tents or small RVs (no hookups), and eight sites for tents only. The camp has a blacktop road and dirt sites, some with patches of grass. There are no spurs; parking is on the sites. The maximum RV length is about 18 feet.

Each campsite has a picnic table and a metal fire ring (with grill). The camp has vault toilets and trash bins, but no water. RV water and dump stations are provided at Tejon Pass Rest Area, on I-5, north of Frazier Park.

Cienaga Campground is usually open from mid-May to September. The camping limit is 14 days.

Caution: The side road leading to camp is a narrow, winding dirt road of more than 5 miles in length that is rocky in places. It is crossed in several places by streams, and by a rocky wash near the camp entrance. It is not recommended for trailers or motorhomes. Signs throughout the area indicate that the dirt roads are not maintained for low-clearance vehicles, but are suitable for jeeps, all-terrain vehicles (ATVs), and motorcycles.

DIRECTIONS From I-5 in Castaic, take Lake Hughes Road east about 13 miles (the road bends northeast). At unpaved Forest Road 6N32, turn left (northwest). Go 6.5 miles to the campground (camp sign missing, as of this writing).

Cottonwood Campground

GENERAL SETTING (LOCATION, FEATURES, SUPPLIES, INFORMATION) Picturesque Elizabeth Lake Canyon, between

Castaic and Lake Hughes, is the setting of this medium-sized national forest campground. The elevation is 2600 feet. Being easily accessible from the highway, this campground is popular with families. It has helped fill a gap left by the closing of Prospect Campground, about 4 miles southwest, where facilities were removed and a sign says CAMPGROUND CLOSED, as of this writing.

Cottonwood trees, for which the camp is named, are found in abundance along the canyon stream that separates the camp from the highway, and give shade to some campsites near the stream. Oaks shade some sites at another part of the camp, and pines at still another. Campsites are set along the camp road that winds through the high-walled canyon, and some sites sit on a slight incline. Short log posts and some bushes separate the campsites.

Elizabeth Lake Day-Use Area is located at beautiful Elizabeth Lake, near a quiet area of country homes, 2.5 miles east of Lake Hughes. It features about a dozen picnic sites situated near the shore with a terrific view of the lake and the chaparral hills across the lake. A few transplanted short pines provide limited shade. Fishing is permitted at the lake, and a boat launch ramp is available. Motorboats with engines under 10 h.p. and sailboats are allowed on the lake, but no jet skis. Swimming is permitted. *Caution:* Trees and fences are submerged in the lake.

The Antelope Valley Poppy Reserve, on Lancaster Road north of Lake Hughes, is a special place set aside for people to enjoy early spring wildflowers in bloom. A visitor center, a picnic area, and hiking trails are provided.

Supplies and gasoline are available in Castaic. Limited supplies are available at Lake Hughes, 4.5 miles northeast of camp. For more information, write or phone the Santa Clara/Mojave Rivers Ranger District Office of the Angeles National Forest.

SITES, FEES, FACILITIES, TIME LIMITS The campground has 22 nonreservable, unnumbered campsites for tents or RVs (no hookups). An Adventure Pass is required for a parked vehicle. The camp has dirt campsites, some with patches of grass. The camp's road and parking spurs are blacktop. The maximum RV length is about 22 feet.

Each campsite has a picnic table and a pedestal barbecue or a metal fire ring (with grill). The camp has vault toilets and a dumpster, but no water. RV water and dump stations are provided at Tejon Pass Rest Area, on I-5, north of Frazier Park.

Elizabeth Lake Day-Use Area has picnic tables, barbecues, wheelchair-accessible vault toilets, trash bins, and a spacious blacktop parking lot. A parked vehicle requires an Adventure Pass.

Cottonwood Campground is usually open all year. The camping limit is 14 days. *Caution:* The stream crosses the camp road just beyond the entrance, and could be hard to cross during rains.

DIRECTIONS From I-5 in Castaic, take Lake Hughes Road east about 18 miles (the road bends northeast). The camp entrance is on the right (south) side of the highway.

Zuni and Streamside Campgrounds

GENERAL SETTING (LOCATION, FEATURES, SUPPLIES, INFORMATION) Both these national forest campgrounds in Bouquet Canyon are streamside camps, though just one camp's name indicates such. Bouquet Canyon Creek, the stream that flows through the canyon, separates the camps from the highway, and fishing is permitted. The two camps, roughly 3 miles apart, are similar in appearance and are set at the foot of the hills that form the canyon's northern wall. The canyon is fairly narrow, almost like a gorge, but the camps easily fit due to their small size.

At Streamside Camp, tall oaks and sycamores shade most sites. Zuni Camp is less shaded. A low, stone retaining wall near the entrance of Streamside Camp adds to the camp's rustic ambience. One drawback is the close proximity of both camps to a growing residential area and a well-traveled highway with traffic noise.

Across the highway near Zuni Camp is Los Cantiles Day-Use Area, with a locked gate and a sign that says ENTRY BY PERMIT ONLY. Only groups are allowed, with priority given to groups with disabilities, and reservations are required. Featured are a braille-signed nature trail and a picnic area that are wheelchair accessible.

The elevation is 1700 feet at Zuni Camp, and 2500 feet at Streamside Camp. Both campgrounds have had to fill in for several other little camps that are closed along Bouquet Canyon Road, including Bouquet, Big Oak, Hollow Tree, Chaparral, and Falls.

Supplies and gasoline are available in Valencia and Santa Clarita. For more information, write or phone the Santa Clara/Mojave Rivers Ranger District Office of the Angeles National Forest.

SITES, FEES, FACILITIES, TIME LIMITS Both campgrounds have nonreservable, unnumbered campsites for tents or RVs (no hookups). Zuni Camp has 10 sites. Streamside Camp has nine sites. A parked vehicle requires an Adventure Pass. Each camp's road and parking spurs are paved. Campsites are dirt with some patches of grass. The maximum RV length is about 22 feet.

At both camps, each site has a picnic table and a metal fire ring (with grill). There are vault toilets and trash cans (no water).

Los Cantiles Day-Use Area, for up to 200 people, has a few picnic tables and barbecues, water, and wheelchair-accessible toilets. Groups with disabilities pay no fee. For other groups, the fee is $75 for 100 people or less, and $150 for between 100 and 200 people. For a permit and reservations, phone the ranger district office.

Zuni Campground and Streamside Campground are usually open from May 1 to November 30. The camping limit is 14 days.

DIRECTIONS From I-5 in Valencia, take Valencia Boulevard east 2.5 miles to Bouquet Canyon Road. Turn left (northeast) and go about 7 miles to Zuni Campground. Go 3.5 miles farther to Streamside Campground (camp sign missing, as of this writing). Both camps are on the left (north) side of the highway.

Spunky Campground

GENERAL SETTING (LOCATION, FEATURES, SUPPLIES, INFORMATION) Spunky is an intriguing name for a canyon, from which this national forest camp gets its name. The name fits the camp too, since camping is for spunky people who crave the rugged outdoors' life. The camp is set on a little oak-shaded flat at the mouth of a small canyon near the village of Green Valley, northeast of Santa Clarita. The elevation at camp is 3300 feet.

At the eastern end of camp is the trailhead of a trail that leads east into the canyon. The Pacific Crest Trail crosses San Francisquito Canyon Road near Green Valley Forest Station, about 3 miles northeast of camp. At times, a camp host resides in camp. South Portal Camp, a few miles away, has been closed.

Supplies and gasoline are available in Valencia and Santa Clarita. Limited supplies and gasoline are available in Green Valley near camp. For more information, contact the Santa Clara/Mojave Rivers Ranger District Office of the Angeles National Forest.

SITES, FEES, FACILITIES, TIME LIMITS The camp has 10 nonreservable numbered campsites for tents or small RVs (no hookups). A parked vehicle requires an Adventure Pass. The camp has a paved loop road. Campsites and parking spurs are dirt. Spurs are rather small; the maximum RV length is about 18 feet.

Each campsite has a picnic table. Each site also has a pedestal barbecue and/or a metal fire ring (with grill). The camp has vault toilets, trash cans, and recycling bins, but no water.

Spunky Campground is usually open from May 1 to November 30. The camping limit is 14 days.

DIRECTIONS From I-5 in Valencia, take Valencia Boulevard east 2.5 miles to Bouquet Canyon Road. Turn left (northeast) and go about 17 miles to Spunky Canyon Road. Turn left (northwest), and go 3.7 miles to the campground on the right (east) side of the road.

Walker Ranch Group Camp

GENERAL SETTING (LOCATION, FEATURES, SUPPLIES, INFORMATION) This primitive camp is open on a limited basis for youth groups such as the Boy Scouts and YMCA Indian Guides. It is part of Placerita Canyon State and County Park, east of Newhall, and is located about 2 miles east of the park's main area. Only tents and one vehicle are allowed at this camp, but no RVs. The main part of the park features a nature center, a museum, a classroom, and a nature trail that help make discovering nature fun and educational.

The park is state-owned, but is operated by Los Angeles County Department of Parks and Recreation through a long-term lease. The park's property originally came from the Walker family in 1949, who had owned it up to that time, hence the camp's name. The family desired that the park be kept in a pristine state.

The camp's dirt access road drops down below the highway toward the edge of a small grassy valley, and reaches a stream beyond which the camp sits, partly shaded by tall oaks. Near the camp are several fairly rugged hiking trails. Canyon Trail leads west to the main part of the park. Los Pinetos Trail goes south a few miles to Wilson Canyon Saddle. Waterfall Trail leads south to a nature trail and a waterfall. Oak Pass Trail connects the camp with Placerita Canyon Road, about a quarter mile north.

Two little Angeles National Forest camps in the area have been redesignated as areas for limited day use. Live Oak Picnic Area, formerly Live Oak Camp, is in an oak glen near Sand Canyon Road, 3.5 miles east of Walker Ranch. The blacktop access road is gated, so walk about 500 feet from the highway. *Caution:* A stream crosses the access road. Soledad Wildlife Viewing Area, formerly Soledad Camp, features interpretive panels. It is set on the north side of Soledad Canyon Road, 1.5 miles east of Agua Dulce Road.

Vasquez Rocks County Park is on Agua Dulce Road, 1.5 miles north of State Route 14. Its jagged stone formations have been filmed in movie and television scenes.

Supplies and gasoline are available in Newhall, Canyon Country, and Santa Clarita. For further information, write or phone Placerita Canyon State and County Park.

SITES, FEES, FACILITIES, TIME LIMITS Three small group campsites accommodate 20 to 25 youths each. The fee is $50 per group site, per night. Each site has picnic tables and metal fire rings (with grills). The camp has benches, drinking fountains, portable chemical toilets, trash cans, and information boards.

A dirt parking area is provided for day use near the stream crossing. Again, only one vehicle (not an RV) is allowed in camp overnight and must be parked at the parking area.

Note: Required at Walker Ranch are a permit, to be filled out and signed, and an insurance policy relieving Los Angeles County of liability; phone for details. Adult supervision is required. An adult is given a key to the campsite and a key to turn on the water. Signs mention that the water is trucked in, limited, and expensive, so please conserve it.

Live Oak Picnic Area has a few picnic tables, metal fire rings (with grills), a pedestal barbecue, a vault toilet, and trash cans; parking outside the gate is limited. Soledad Wildlife Viewing Area has a few picnic tables, drinking fountains, benches, a vault toilet, and a trash can. Some picnic sites at Soledad are on concrete slabs with concrete paths; these sites and the vault toilet are wheelchair accessible. At both day-use areas, a parked vehicle requires an Adventure Pass.

Caution: At Walker Ranch Group Camp, signs warn hikers to stay on trails to avoid rattlesnakes, and warn that vehicles should not be driven on the camp's dirt roads during rains.

DIRECTIONS From I-5 in Newhall, take State Route 14 (Antelope Valley Freeway) northeast about 3 miles to Placerita Canyon Road. Exit and turn right (east). Go 1.4 miles and pass Placerita Canyon State and County Park's main entrance, then go about 2 miles to unpaved Walker Ranch Road. If the gate is open, turn right (south) and go about half a mile to the campground.

LOS ANGELES COUNTY MOUNTAIN AREA

LITTLEROCK RESERVOIR AREA AND MOUNT GLEASON AREA

1. Saddleback Butte State Park
2. Rocky Point Campground
3. Sage Campground
4. Messenger Flats Campground
5. Lightning Point Group Camp
6. Monte Cristo Campground

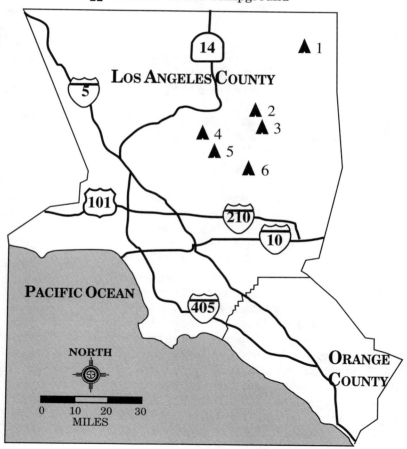

29

Saddleback Butte State Park

GENERAL SETTING (LOCATION, FEATURES, SUPPLIES, INFORMATION) Colorful wildflowers during spring attract visitors to the Antelope Valley. Campsites at this desert valley's state park are naturally decorated by the flowers at that time. The antelopes, for which the valley was named, are history now. Joshua trees are scattered over the flats surrounding Saddleback Butte, but the butte is fairly bare, with little brush on it. The presence of this state park of nearly 3000 acres has helped keep the area and the trees around the butte in a natural, unspoiled state.

True to its name, the butte has a dip in its ridge like that of a saddle. The butte is part of a range of hills, and is connected to another butte, north of the park, by a very wide, low dip in the hills. This wide dip is traversed by Avenue J near the park. Seen from camp, the butte dominates the skyline to the east, at an elevation of 3651 feet. Saddleback Butte Trail leads from camp to the butte. Phone for fees and special rules regarding the 4.5-mile horseback riding trail which goes along the base of the butte.

This state park is located north of the small residential community of Wilsona Gardens, and is roughly 20 miles east of Lancaster and Littlerock. The park's elevation, around the base of the butte, is about 2700 feet. Since the park's public campground is the only one in the Antelope Valley, it is included with the Littlerock Reservoir Area in this book, for convenience.

The park's primitive desert campground features family campsites set among typical desert bushes such as creosotes. The group campsite, north of the family camping area, can be found easily due to an exceptionally tall Joshua tree guarding its entrance. The campfire center has benches and a concrete fire ring. At times, a camp host is present. Desert summers can be very hot, and winters cold, even freezing at times. Spring and fall are pleasant.

The park's picnic area is situated on a rise at the edge of the foothills, about a mile north of camp, via the park's dirt access road. Picnic sites are set among Joshua trees and creosote bushes.

The visitor center sits on a knoll, south of the picnic area. A trail leads south from the picnic area down into the valley about 200 feet to the vault toilet structures. The trail continues west about the same distance up the knoll to the visitor center, situated near natural rock piles. From there, the half-mile nature trail leads west, farther up the knoll, to a good view of the park and the valley. Interpretive panels are provided.

The park has a view of the Antelope Valley to the south with the San Gabriel Mountains in the distance, snowcapped during winter. Piute Butte can be seen in the foreground, and is where the Antelope Valley Indian Museum is located. Native American history and culture are the themes of this museum on Avenue M, 3.5 miles southwest of the state park. The unusual, chalet-style museum building has Native American paintings on its outside walls and is built into the rock at the foot of Piute Butte, which is reached by Piute Butte Nature Trail. The museum is open on weekends most of the year, but is closed during summer.

The BLM's El Mirage OHV Area, roughly 10 miles southeast of the park, is north of El Mirage Road and the community of El Mirage. This 24,000-acre OHV area features a dry lake bed.

Supplies and gasoline are available in Lancaster. Limited supplies, gasoline, and a pay phone are available at Lake Los Angeles, about 4 miles south of camp (the lake is usually dry). For more information, write or phone Saddleback Butte State Park.

SITES, FEES, FACILITIES, TIME LIMITS The campground has 50 nonreservable, unnumbered family campsites for tents or RVs (no hookups). The nightly fee is $8 per site. Camp roads, parking spurs, and campsites are dirt and sand. Small concrete curb sections outline parking spurs and separate campsites. The maximum RV length is about 30 feet.

Each family campsite has a picnic table and a pedestal barbecue. Some sites have a ramada and a concrete or metal fire ring.

The group campsite accommodates 30 people and 12 vehicles. Vehicles may include two RVs, but no trailers. Tents are allowed. The nightly fee for the group site is $22, and reservations are required. The group site, road, and parking area are sand and dirt; parking is limited. The maximum RV length is about 24 feet.

The group campsite has two large ramadas, picnic tables, pedestal barbecues, and a large, bowl-shaped barbecue.

The campground has water spigots, drinking fountains, an RV water and dump station, trash cans, and an information board. The camp's restrooms have sinks, flush toilets (some with wheelchair access), electrical outlets, and lights.

The picnic area has picnic tables, pedestal barbecues, some ramadas, vault toilets nearby (see above), trash bins, and a dirt road. The day-use parking fee is $2 per vehicle.

No OHV use is permitted in the park. Camping is allowed only in the campground, which is usually open. At family sites, the camping limit is 14 days. At the group site, the limit is seven days.

DIRECTIONS From State Route 14 (freeway) in Lancaster, take Avenue J (County Highway N-5) east about 19 miles to 170th Street East. Turn right (south) and go about a mile to Avenue K. Turn left (east) and go 500 feet to the camp entrance. Turn left (north).

Rocky Point and Sage Campgrounds

GENERAL SETTING (LOCATION, FEATURES, SUPPLIES, INFORMATION) The Littlerock Recreation Area, southeast of Palmdale, includes these two campgrounds. Though part of the Angeles National Forest, this does not look like a typical forest area. Instead of mountain pines, desert Joshua trees predominate along the road to the recreation area and at a few spots inside. After passing the entrance station, the road wanders through a canyon with low, barren walls, and then approaches Littlerock Reservoir, shimmering like a jewel in the sunlight. A lookout point affords a view of the dam and spillway to the east, and of the reservoir to the south. The pine-clad San Gabriel Mountains, which can be seen to the south, contrast with the barren hills surrounding the reservoir. Farther down the road, an inviting, tree-shaded cove for fishing is passed, then Fishermans Point.

The camps are situated near each other on the west side of the reservoir and are very small tent camps. At both campgrounds, the road passes next to the bare hills of the canyon. The camps sit in small places between the road and reservoir, a few feet above the water. Sage Camp sits a little higher above the reservoir, and its campsites are farther apart. It takes its name from the desert vegetation on the adjacent hill. Oaks, Joshua trees, and chaparral can be seen on nearby hills to the south. One of Sage's campsites is down an inclined dirt path closer to the water. There is not much shoreline at either camp—the bluff drops abruptly into the water. Fishing is allowed, but there is more room at the day-use areas. Both camps have views of the lake. The trees nearby do not shade the camps, so ramadas are provided. The elevation is 3400 feet at both camps.

Juniper Picnic Area and the Littlerock Boat Launch parking lot are next to each other, in the area where Juniper Grove Camp and Lakeside Camp once were. The picnic area has a view of the reservoir. The boat launch parking lot has plenty of room for vehicles parked for daytime fishing. A small store is across the road (see below). An OHV trail near the store leads west into the hills.

Motorboats with engines under 10 h.p. and sailboats are permitted on the reservoir. No swimming is allowed.

The Littlerock Creek area, south of the reservoir, is closed at this time for the protection of endangered species. An 11-mile stretch of Forest Road 5N04, a rough dirt road for four-wheel-drive vehicles, is closed in that area, from a quarter mile south of Sage Camp to Sulphur Springs Group Camp. The closed area includes much of the Littlerock OHV Area, including Alimony Ridge and Santiago Canyon OHV routes; phone for updates. Basin Campground in that area is also closed. Near the closed area, at Forest Road 5N04D to Joshua Tree Camp, a sign says CAMPGROUND CLOSED FOR RELIEF AND REHABILITATION. This camp, situated on a shelf jutting toward the reservoir, is now mainly home to the trees it was named after.

The store across the road from Juniper Picnic Area has boat rentals, bait, tackle, firewood, gifts, a snack bar, and a pay phone. Supplies and gasoline are available in Palmdale. Limited supplies are available in Littlerock, roughly 10 miles northeast.

For additional information, write or phone the Mojave Work Center of the Angeles National Forest.

SITES, FEES, FACILITIES, TIME LIMITS Rocky Point Camp has three tent sites, and Sage Camp has four tent sites. All sites are nonreservable. At both camps, the nightly fee is $10 per site or the display of an Adventure Pass plus $5. A vehicle parked for day use in the Littlerock Recreation Area requires an Adventure Pass. Rocky Point has wheelchair-accessible campsites set on concrete slabs next to concrete paths. Sage has dirt sites next to concrete paths. Each camp has a small blacktop parking lot near the sites.

At both camps, each site has a picnic table, a metal fire ring (with grill), and a ramada. Sites at Rocky Point also have a pedestal barbecue. Both camps have wheelchair-accessible vault toilets and a dumpster. During summer, Rocky Point has piped water.

Juniper Picnic Area has tables, pedestal barbecues, ramadas, vault toilets, and a dumpster. Fishermans Point and the Littlerock Boat Launch area each have a blacktop parking lot, a dumpster, and vault toilets. The lookout at the dam has interpretive panels, a shelter, two benches, a concrete path, and a dirt parking area nearby. Most day-use facilities are wheelchair accessible.

Rocky Point and Sage Campgrounds are usually open from mid-April to October. The camping limit is 14 days.

DIRECTIONS From State Route 14 (freeway) in Palmdale, exit at State Highway 138. Go east about 8 miles to Cheeseboro Road, and turn right (south). Go about 3 miles to the entrance station, and the road becomes Forest Road 5N04. Go 2 miles to Rocky Point Camp then a short way to Sage Camp; both are on the road's left (east) side. Local signs say LITTLEROCK DAM AND RECREATION FACILITY.

Messenger Flats Campground

GENERAL SETTING (LOCATION, FEATURES, SUPPLIES, INFORMATION) As Mount Gleason Road ascends higher into the pines, and wanders just below the ridge of the mountain, breathtaking views to the north are experienced from points along the road. Aliso Canyon is in the foreground with Soledad Canyon behind, and the Antelope Valley in the far distance. There are views of the San Gabriel Mountains to the south from some points, including Mount Wilson with its television towers and observatory dome, which appears as a speck from more than 10 miles away.

The Mount Gleason area lies within the Angeles National Forest, and is northeast of Tujunga. At Messenger Flats Campground, a primitive tent camp that is not far from Mount Gleason Road, the elevation is 5500 feet. The camp's access road ends at camp and a dirt parking area lined with pole fences. You must park and walk a few yards to the campsites, which go up the side of a low hill, not far from the top. At the top, there is a partial view to the south. Campsites are fairly well shaded by pines. For equestrians, the campground features two horse corrals and hitching rails.

The Mount Gleason area has some signs of civilization. The campground is 1.5 miles west of Mount Gleason summit (elevation: 6532 feet) with its microwave relay station, and is a few miles west of Fire Camp 16, a conservation camp.

The Pacific Crest Trail passes by the campground. It parallels and crosses Mount Gleason Road at some points, between Mill Creek Summit and North Fork Saddle. A trailhead with a parking lot, near Mill Creek Summit, is on Forest Road 3N17, east of Angeles Forest Highway. From this trailhead, Big Buck Trail Camp, a hike-in camp, is about 5 miles west on the Pacific Crest Trail. From this trailhead, an OHV route (4N18) leads south. Fishing is permitted down in Mill Creek.

Mill Creek Summit Picnic Area, at Mill Creek Summit, is partly shaded by trees. This picnic area and Big Buck Trail Camp have hitching rails for horses. An information board at the picnic area describes the Big Tujunga Canyon auto tour along Big Tujunga Canyon Road and Angeles Forest Highway.

Aliso Springs Picnic Area, half a mile north of Mill Creek Summit, is very small, tucked in a heavily shaded spot where the foot of a hill meets Angeles Forest Highway. Parking is limited.

About 5 miles east of camp is Forest Road 4N24 for ORV use and Penny Pines wildlife viewing area. Penny Pines refers to children's contributions to the planting of pines in the national forest.

Supplies and gasoline are available in La Cañada. For additional information, write or phone the Little Tujunga Work Center of the Angeles National Forest.

SITES, FEES, FACILITIES, TIME LIMITS The camp has 10 nonreservable tent sites. The nightly fee is $10 per site. The camp's road and sites are dirt. The camp has a dirt parking area (no spurs).

Each campsite has a picnic table and a metal fire ring (with grill). The camp has vault toilets, trash bins, and an information board. Piped water is available during some summers.

Mill Creek Picnic Area is wheelchair accessible. It has picnic tables, pedestal barbecues, vault toilets, information boards, trash cans, and a parking lot. Aliso Springs Picnic Area has two tables, a pedestal barbecue, a vault toilet, and a trash can. Besides hitching rails, Big Buck Trail Camp has some grills, but no water, tables, or toilets. At the Pacific Crest Trail blacktop parking lot east of Angeles Forest Highway, facilities include a drinking fountain, vault toilets, hitching rails, and trash cans.

A vehicle parked at a picnic area or at a trailhead of a trail camp requires an Adventure Pass.

Messenger Flats Camp is open from April to October. The camping limit is 14 days. *Caution:* The roads to camp are winding, with some dirt stretches that are narrow.

DIRECTIONS From I-210 in La Cañada, take State Highway 2 (Angeles Crest Highway) north about 9 miles to County Highway N-3 (Angeles Forest Highway). Turn left (northwest) and go 14.5 miles to Forest Road 3N17 (Mount Gleason Road) at Mill Creek Summit. Turn left (west) and go 6 miles to a fork. Bear left and continue straight ahead (west) on 3N17, which becomes dirt. Go half a mile and the road becomes blacktop. Go 2 miles to another fork. Bear left and continue straight ahead (west) on 3N17. Go half a mile to a crossroad, which leads north to Messenger Flats Campground and south to Lightning Point Group Camp.

Messenger Flats: At the crossroad, bear right (north) on 3N17, which becomes dirt. Go a mile to the dirt access road. Turn left (south); go 500 feet to Messenger Flats Camp's dirt parking area.

Lightning Point: At the crossroad, turn left (south) on Forest Road 3N32 (dirt). Go a quarter mile to a fork where paved Forest Road 3N32B is on the left, and if the gate is open, bear left (southwest). Go about half a mile to Lightning Point Group Camp.

Lightning Point Group Camp

GENERAL SETTING (LOCATION, FEATURES, SUPPLIES, INFORMATION) This group camp is situated in a stunning pine forest in the Mount Gleason area of the Angeles National Forest. The elevation is 5900 feet. The camp has access to the Pacific Crest Trail. For more on the area, see Messenger Flats Campground.

Group campsites are grouped in pairs, close to the top of a hump-shaped hill. Corrals and a parking lot are at the top of the hill. Only tent camping is allowed. Each pair of campsites is spaced well apart from the others in clearings surrounded by pines. Sites 1 and 2 are the farthest from the parking lot, and are on a fairly level spot on the west side of camp where the camp road ends. These campsites have views of the hills to the south and west. Sites 3 and 4 are on the north side of camp. They have limited views, through the trees, of the neighboring pine-clad hills. Sites 5 and 6, on the east side of camp, are very close to the hilltop and are near the corrals. They have views of the hills to east and the relay station. Most campsites have a campfire circle, but sites 5 and 6 share one, to the south. Each campfire circle has a metal fire ring (without grill) and logs split in half that serve as benches.

Trail Canyon Trail leads southwest from camp about 9 miles to Big Tujunga Canyon Road. Tom Lucas Trail Camp is on this trail; three picnic areas are near the road. For more on the trail camp and picnic areas, see Monte Cristo Campground in this book.

Supplies and gasoline are available in La Cañada. For required group reservations and other information, write or phone the Little Tujunga Work Center of the Angeles National Forest.

SITES, FEES, FACILITIES, TIME LIMITS There are six group tent sites. Each site accommodates 40 people; the entire camp accommodates 240 people. The nightly fee is $40 per site, or $240 for the whole camp. Reservations are required. The camp road is mostly blacktop, but is unpaved near the corrals; sites are dirt. The parking lot is blacktop; the maximum RV length is 24 feet.

Each group site has a few picnic tables, a large pedestal barbecue, and trash cans. Each pair of sites shares two flush toilets (some with wheelchair access). At times, piped water is available.

Lightning Point Group Camp is usually open from May to October. The camping limit is 14 days. *Caution:* The roads to camp are winding, with some dirt stretches that are narrow.

DIRECTIONS See directions for Messenger Flats Campground.

Monte Cristo Campground

GENERAL SETTING (LOCATION, FEATURES, SUPPLIES, INFORMATION) In the bottom of a beautiful canyon with its chaparral-blanketed walls, sits this nice little campground. It is close to the highway and is situated about 50 feet below it, near the fork of Monte Cristo Creek and Mill Creek. Fishing is permitted. Some campsites are partly shaded by sycamores and oaks. The elevation at this primitive national forest camp is 3600 feet.

Monte Cristo Camp is located north of La Cañada, 1.5 miles north of Monte Cristo Forest Station and 2.5 miles north of Hidden Springs. Hidden Springs Picnic Area is located north of a tunnel, close to a sheer cliff in a narrow canyon with a stream and a few pines. Fall Creek Trail Camp, a hike-in camp, is a few miles west of Hidden Springs, and is reached by Fall Creek Trail, 600 feet north of Hidden Springs Picnic Area. Schoening Springs Picnic Area (two sites) is located 3.5 miles south of camp in a small cove at the foot of a hill next to the highway, and is well shaded.

If you drive to the mountains through Big Tujunga Canyon, fishing and three more picnic areas await you. From Big Tujunga Canyon Road, about 6 miles northeast of Tujunga, steep Doske Road leads south a short way down to Wildwood Picnic Area in the bottom of the canyon. Oaks and scrub pines afford some shade. About a mile west of Wildwood, a dirt road leads north from Big Tujunga Canyon Road to the trailhead of Trail Canyon Trail. This trail leads northeast about 9 miles to Lightning Point Group Camp (open from May to October). Tom Lucas Trail Camp, a tiny hike-in camp with hitching rails, is a few miles north of the trailhead.

From Big Tujunga Canyon Road, about a mile east of Wildwood Picnic Area, Vogel Flat Road leads south a short way to Stonyvale Road and to Stonyvale and Vogel Flats Picnic Areas. Wheelchair-accessible Stonyvale Picnic Area lies at a narrow place in the canyon near Big Tujunga River, where fishing is permitted. Stonyvale Picnic Area is partly shaded by oaks.

Vogel Flats Picnic Area, at one time a campground, is now designated for day use only. Partly shaded by scattered oaks, it occupies a wide spot in the chaparral-clad canyon. *Vogel* means *bird*, in German, and is related to the English word *fowl*. It is a good choice for the name of a woodland picnic area and former campground, where birds can still be heard singing in the trees.

A few miles east of Vogel Flats, the highway reaches the Big Tujunga Dam Overlook with a view of the 1931 dam and the river; there are interpretive panels, a bench, and a blacktop parking lot.

Supplies and gasoline are available in La Cañada, roughly 20 miles south of camp, and in Palmdale, by taking Angeles Forest Highway north from camp about 15 miles to Sierra Highway, then taking Sierra Highway north about 5 miles. A pay phone is available at Hidden Springs, 2.5 miles south of camp.

For additional information, write or phone the Little Tujunga Work Center of the Angeles National Forest.

SITES, FEES, FACILITIES, TIME LIMITS Monte Cristo Camp has 19 nonreservable, numbered campsites for tents or RVs (no hookups). The nightly fee is $8 per site. The camp road and spurs are blacktop. Most campsites are dirt. Two concrete campsites are wheelchair accessible. The maximum RV length is about 30 feet.

Each campsite has a picnic table. Most sites have a metal fire ring (with grill); wheelchair sites have a pedestal barbecue. The camp has water spigots, vault toilets (some with wheelchair access), information boards, trash cans, and a blacktop parking lot.

The four picnic areas have picnic tables, pedestal barbecues, information boards, and trash cans. Vogel Flats also has metal fire rings (with grills) and flush toilets, Schoening Springs has no toilets, and the other picnic areas have vault toilets. At Schoening Springs, parking is limited to the dirt strip next to the highway. The other picnic areas have blacktop parking lots. Stonyvale has blacktop paths and a few tables set on concrete slabs; these and some vault toilets are wheelchair accessible.

Fall Creek Trail Camp has six sites, and Tom Lucas Trail Camp has two sites. These hike-in camps have some picnic tables and grills, but no water. Fall Creek Trail Camp has vault toilets.

A vehicle parked at a picnic area or at a trailhead of a trail camp requires an Adventure Pass.

Monte Cristo Campground is usually open all year. The camping limit is 14 days. *Caution:* The camp road is crossed by streams.

DIRECTIONS From I-210 in La Cañada, take State Highway 2 (Angeles Crest Highway) north about 9 miles to County Highway N-3 (Angeles Forest Highway). Turn left (northwest) and go nearly 10 miles to the access road. Turn right (east) and go to camp.

LOS ANGELES COUNTY MOUNTAIN AREA

MOUNT WILSON AREA, CHILAO AREA, AND CRYSTAL LAKE AREA

▲ 1. Millard Camp
▲ 2. Chilao Camp
▲ 3. Coulter Group Camp
▲ 4. Horse Flats Camp
▲ 5. Bandido Group Camp
▲ 6. Mount Pacifico Camp

▲ 7. Sulphur Springs Group Camp
▲ 8. Buckhorn Camp
▲ 9. Coldbrook Camp
▲10. Crystal Lake Camp
▲11. Deer Flats Group Camp

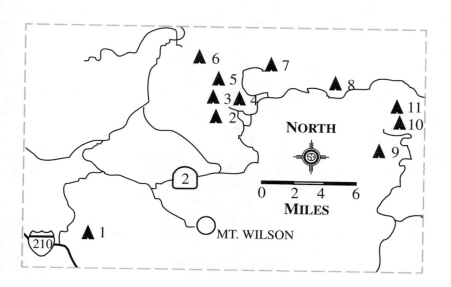

Millard Campground

GENERAL SETTING (LOCATION, FEATURES, SUPPLIES, INFORMATION) This small, primitive walk-in camp is located in the Angeles National Forest, north of Altadena, at an elevation of 1900 feet. The camp sits by a stream in narrow Millard Canyon, and is well shaded by oaks and riparian trees. From Chaney Trail, the paved vehicular road into the area, there are views of Altadena on a clear day. Millard Canyon Falls Trail is near camp.

Clear Creek Information Station, open during summer, serves the Mount Wilson area. It is located on Angeles Crest Highway (State Highway 2) at Angeles Forest Highway (County Highway N-3), about 9 miles north of La Cañada and 4.5 miles west of Mount Wilson Road and Red Box Gap.

Switzer Picnic Area, east of Clear Creek Information Station, is set at the bottom of a narrow canyon shaded by oaks and sycamores. Picnic sites sit on both sides of a creek, with footbridges crossing it. Parking lots serve the picnic area and trailheads. There is access to Nature Canteen Trail and to Gabrielino and Silver Moccasin Trails, two national recreation trails. Gabrielino Trail leads south about a mile to Switzer Falls and about 5 miles to Oakwilde Trail Camp. It leads east 4.5 miles to Red Box Picnic Area near Red Box Gap (see below). *Caution:* Switzer Picnic Area has a winding access road; a sign says NARROW STEEP ROAD.

Gabrielino Trail also follows Arroyo Seco Canyon, north of Pasadena. A trailhead and a blacktop parking lot are on Highway 2 in a residential area, about 2 miles north of I-210. From there, Forest Road 2N69 (closed to vehicles) leads east about a mile to Gould Mesa Trail Camp and Gabrielino Trail, on which are two tiny picnic areas, a few miles north, and Oakwilde Trail Camp, several miles north. Several miles farther north is Switzer Picnic Area.

Mount Wilson affords impressive views of the San Gabriel Valley to the south and Los Angeles in the distance, when visibility is clear. An observatory, television towers, and a small picnic area are at the top, at the end of Mount Wilson Road, about 4 miles south of Highway 2. At the junction of Mount Wilson Road and Highway 2, near Red Box Gap, are little Red Box Picnic Area and the American Indian Cultural Center (open on a limited basis). Horse corrals and hitching rails are provided. Red Box Picnic Area's east side is shaded by pines and has a view of Mount Baldy; the west side is shaded by oaks. From the picnic area, Gabrielino Trail leads west 4.5 miles to Switzer Picnic Area.

Valley Forge Trail Camp and West Fork Trail Camp are hike-in camps that used to be road camps. The trailhead is on Mount Wilson Road, just south of Highway 2. Forest Road 2N24 (closed to vehicles) leads southeast about 2 miles to Valley Forge Trail Camp and 5.5 miles to West Fork Trail Camp. Other trail camps in the Mount Wilson area require lengthy hikes of several miles.

Chantry Flat Picnic Area and Chantry Flat Information Station (open weekends) are located at the end of Big Santa Anita Canyon Road, 4.5 miles north of Arcadia. The road rises high up into the hills with views of the San Gabriel Valley and Santa Anita Canyon; there are steep dropoffs. The picnic area is set on the side of a somewhat steep hill above the access road, and is well shaded by oaks. Dirt footpaths are provided. A snack bar and a pack station for horses are nearby. Fishing is permitted in Santa Anita Creek. Upper Winter Creek Trail (2N41), a fire road closed to vehicles, leads northwest about 3 miles to Hoegees Trail Camp and about 7 miles to Mount Wilson. Gabrielino Trail leads north 2 miles to Sturtevant Falls and 4 miles to Spruce Grove Trail Camp.

Supplies and gasoline are available in Pasadena, Altadena, Arcadia, and La Cañada. For information, contact the Los Angeles River Ranger District Office of the Angeles National Forest.

SITES, FEES, FACILITIES, TIME LIMITS Millard Campground has five nonreservable, walk-in dirt campsites for tents. Before you walk in, an Adventure Pass must be displayed on your parked vehicle. A sign says SELECT SITE AND SEE HOST BEFORE SETTING UP CAMP.

Each site has a picnic table and a pedestal barbecue. The camp has a vault toilet, trash cans, and an information board (no water).

Switzer, Red Box, and Chantry Flat Picnic Areas have picnic tables, pedestal barbecues, trash cans (or bins), and blacktop parking lots. Switzer has water spigots and vault toilets. Red Box has a drinking fountain, flush toilets, and a dumpster. Chantry Flat has drinking fountains, water spigots, and restrooms with sinks and flush toilets (some with wheelchair access). Pay phones are located at Red Box Picnic Area (west side) and near Chantry Flat Information Station. A parked vehicle requires an Adventure Pass.

Gould Mesa Trail Camp has three sites, Oakwilde Trail Camp has seven sites, West Fork Trail Camp has seven sites, and Spruce Grove Trail Camp has seven sites. The larger camps are Valley Forge Trail Camp with 12 sites and Hoegees Trail Camp with 15 sites. Each of the six hike-in camps has picnic tables, grills, and vault toilets, but no piped water. Gould Mesa, Oakwilde, Valley Forge, and Hoegees Trail Camps have hitching rails. An Adventure Pass is required for a vehicle parked at a trail camp's trailhead.

Millard Campground is usually open throughout the year. The camping limit is 14 days.

DIRECTIONS From I-210 in northern Pasadena, exit at Lincoln Avenue, and go north about 2 miles to Loma Alta Drive in Altadena. Follow the signs. Turn right (east) and go about half a mile to Chaney Trail, a paved vehicular road. Turn left (north) and go about a mile to Forest Road 2N65. Turn left (west) and go about half a mile to the trailhead parking lot. On the fire road (closed to vehicles), walk north about 500 feet to Millard Campground.

Chilao Campground and Coulter Group Camp

GENERAL SETTING (LOCATION, FEATURES, SUPPLIES, INFORMATION) The Charlton-Chilao Recreation Area, a part of the Angeles National Forest, is located northeast of Mount Wilson. The recreation area includes Chilao Campground, Coulter Group Camp, Chilao Picnic Area, Charlton Flat Picnic Area, Chilao Visitor Center, and Chilao Forest Station.

Chilao Campground (elevation: 5300 feet) is divided into three loops, each with its own entrance. Little Pines Loop and Manzanita Loop occupy rolling terrain on wide ridges with views at some spots of the valley and chaparral hills. Sites are nicely spaced, and manzanita bushes afford privacy; pines shade some sites. Meadow Loop, more primitive than the other loops, is set in a meadowlike depression with sites on either side of a streambed. The camp has walk-in tent sites, some shaded by pines, and has an amphitheater with benches and two stone-concrete fire rings.

Coulter Group Camp is set in an open clearing surrounded by chaparral and a few pines, and is at the back of Manzanita Loop.

At Chilao Visitor Center, visitors are introduced to the forest through exhibits and activities. It is about a mile north of the campgrounds, off State Highway 2, and is open on weekends when the weather permits. During summer, naturalists conduct nature walks, and Saturday evening campfire programs are given at the amphitheater. Special activities are planned for children.

Chilao Picnic Area is next to the visitor center. From the trailhead parking area, about half a mile west of Chilao Picnic Area, Silver Moccasin Trail leads a mile north to Horse Flats Camp.

From the trailhead parking area on Highway 2, Devils Canyon Trail leads a few miles southeast into the San Gabriel Wilderness.

Charlton Flat Picnic Area has more than 175 picnic sites in the pine-forested hills, 2 miles south of Chilao. The access road goes west beyond the picnic area to Vetter Fire Lookout, with parking for views along the way. There is parking along Highway 2 for views of Mount Baldy to the east and Mount Wilson to the south.

At times, Little Pines Loop has a camp host. Supplies and gasoline are available in La Cañada, the last major point before driving more than 20 miles through the mountains to the camps. For required group reservations and other information, write or phone the Little Tujunga Work Center of the Angeles National Forest.

SITES, FEES, FACILITIES, TIME LIMITS Chilao Campground has more than 100 nonreservable family campsites. Little Pines and Manzanita Loops each have about 40 numbered sites for tents or RVs (no hookups). Meadow Loop has about 20 unnumbered tent sites. The nightly fee is $12 per site and $24 per double site.

All campsites are dirt. At Little Pines and Manzanita, loop roads and spurs are blacktop, some spurs are not level, some spurs are pull-throughs, and some sites grouped in threes share small parking lots. The maximum RV length is about 40 feet. Meadow Loop has a blacktop road and small blacktop parking lots (no spurs).

Most sites have a picnic table and a metal fire ring (with or without grill). Some sites have a pedestal or stone barbecue. There are water spigots, vault toilets (some with wheelchair access), dumpsters, and information boards. A pay phone is at Little Pines.

Coulter Group Camp has one group site for tents (not RVs), that accommodates 50 people for $100 per night. The site has picnic tables, a brick barbecue, a water spigot, vault toilets (one with wheelchair access), a dumpster, and a small blacktop parking lot.

An RV dump station is available on State Highway 2, about 2 miles south of the camps, near Charlton Flat Picnic Area.

Chilao and Charlton Flat Picnic Areas have picnic tables, barbecues, vault toilets, trash bins, and blacktop parking lots; Charlton Flat also has fire rings. A pay phone is at Charlton Flat and at Chilao Forest Station. A parked vehicle requires an Adventure Pass. Chilao Picnic Area and its access road were closed at the time of this writing, so facility information was not verifiable on site.

Chilao Campground and Coulter Group Camp are usually open from May to November. The camping limit is 14 days. *Caution:* The road has a stream crossing. Signs say this is bear country.

DIRECTIONS From I-210 in La Cañada, take State Highway 2 (Angeles Crest Highway) north about 25 miles to Chilao Road. Turn left (west) and go 0.25 mile to Forest Road 3N21B, which leads south to Little Pines Loop. Go 0.25 mile to the road that leads south to Manzanita Loop and Coulter Group Camp. Go 0.5 mile to Forest Road 3N14C, which leads south to Meadow Loop.

Horse Flats Campground and Bandido Group Camp

GENERAL SETTING (LOCATION, FEATURES, SUPPLIES, INFORMATION) These primitive national forest camps are located about a mile apart, near the Charlton-Chilao Recreation Area, north of Chilao. The elevation at the campgrounds is 5700 feet.

Of the two campgrounds, Horse Flats has a more natural, less-manicured appearance, with clusters of pines and scrub trees. The access road travels through a narrow canyon that is not too deep. The canyon widens into a small bowl at the campground, where a stream flows next to some sites, and some sites are shaded. The campfire center has benches and a large fire ring. For equestrians, the camp has hitching rails and three corrals.

Bandido Group Camp is attractive and set in a shallow bowl-shaped depression a short way from Forest Road 3N17. The camp is nicely pine-shaded. The main part of the group campsite sits in a dirt clearing on a slight incline next to a stream at the bottom of the bowl, and is surrounded by pines. Some tables and barbecues, south of the main part of the site, are near the campfire circle, which has benches and a large fire ring. There are a few small sites; those near the corrals are in a somewhat overgrown spot.

Bandido Group Camp has a self-guided nature trail. For equestrians, there are corrals, water troughs, and hitching rails.

A parking lot for Silver Moccasin Trail and the Pacific Crest Trail is on Forest Road 3N17, west of State Highway 2. Silver Moccasin Trail, a national recreation trail, passes near Bandido Group Camp and Horse Flats Camp, and goes south about a mile to the Chilao area. Less than a mile west of Horse Flats, another trail (3N14) goes south from Forest Road 3N17 several miles to the Chilao area. For more on the area, see Chilao Camp.

Supplies and gasoline are available in La Cañada, before driving more than 25 miles through the mountains to the camps. For required group reservations and other information, write or phone the Little Tujunga Work Center of the Angeles National Forest.

SITES, FEES, FACILITIES, TIME LIMITS Horse Flats Campground has 24 nonreservable, numbered family campsites for tents or RVs (no hookups). The nightly fee is $12 per site. The camp has a blacktop loop road and dirt campsites, some with grass. Parking spurs are dirt; some spurs are not level. Some sites share small dirt parking areas and require a short walk to reach them. The maximum RV length is about 36 feet. Most campsites have a picnic table and a metal fire ring (with or without grill) or a pedestal barbecue, or both. The camp has vault toilets, information boards, and dumpsters. Piped water is available during some summers.

Bandido Group Camp has one group campsite for tents and RVs, and it accommodates 120 people for $200 per night. The fee for half the group site, 60 people, is $100 per night. The group site has picnic tables, pedestal barbecues, water spigots, vault toilets, information boards, and dumpsters. The loop road and parking lot are blacktop. Each small site has a picnic table and a barbecue.

An RV dump station is available on State Highway 2, 7.5 miles south of the campgrounds, and is near Charlton Flat Picnic Area. Dumpsters are provided along Santa Clara Divide Road (3N17).

The two campgrounds are usually open from April to November. The camping limit is 14 days. *Caution:* Bandido's loop road has a stream crossing. A sign says that this is bear country.

DIRECTIONS From I-210 in La Cañada, take State Highway 2 (Angeles Crest Highway) north about 28 miles to Santa Clara Divide Road (Forest Road 3N17). Turn left (west) and go about 2 miles to Forest Road 3N17E. Turn left (south) and go a short distance to Bandido Group Camp. On Santa Clara Divide Road (Forest Road 3N17), go half a mile farther to Forest Road 3N17G. Turn left (south) and go about half a mile to Horse Flats Campground.

Mount Pacifico Campground and Sulphur Springs Group Camp

GENERAL SETTING (LOCATION, FEATURES, SUPPLIES, INFORMATION) These primitive national forest camps are located about 6 miles apart, north of Chilao. The elevation is 7100 feet at Mount Pacifico Camp, and 5200 feet at Sulphur Springs Camp.

Mount Pacifico Campground sits close to the top of Pacifico Mountain, and is reached by a rocky access road that gradually rises into the pines. The mountaintop is rounded, somewhat like neighboring Round Top, a mountain that is a few miles southwest and can be seen from various points along the access road. The small camp has well-spaced campsites, with some in pairs. Some sites are shaded by pines. Boulders are scattered over the mountaintop and give privacy at some campsites. Yuccas and lupines appear in the region during spring. If you drive to camp from Angeles Forest Highway, there are views along the road of Soledad Canyon, the Littlerock Reservoir, and the Antelope Valley to the north, and of Mount Gleason to the west. Mount Wilson and its observatory and television towers can be seen to the south from the access road. The Pacific Crest Trail crosses the access road about halfway between Forest Road 3N17 and the campground.

Sulphur Springs Group Camp is set in a primitive, natural setting north of the Charlton-Chilao Recreation Area. The access road beyond the gate gradually descends toward the bottom of the canyon. Pines cover the canyon's south wall, and chaparral blankets the north wall. The road is paved for about half a mile, then becomes dirt near the vault toilets. Three small sites are passed. The stream crosses the road, then the canyon and stream bend to the left (north). The road turns right (south) and passes a water trough. It turns right (west) and goes along the south side of the canyon, a quarter mile to the group campsite at the road's end. The site is lightly shaded by pines, and sits on slightly inclined terrain at the foot of the canyon's south wall. The stream separates the group campsite from the vault toilets.

Back at the gate to Sulphur Springs Group Camp, there is a dirt trailhead parking area for day use. A short distance beyond the gate, the camp's access road passes a trail that goes a few yards south to the Pacific Crest Trail, which in turn goes east along the south side of the canyon. From the access road, about half a mile farther, near the vault toilets, another short trail is passed. It leads east, crosses the stream, passes near a water trough, and joins the Pacific Crest Trail as it bends south and goes a few miles to the blacktop trailhead parking lot near State Highway 2.

Granite Mountain and Round Top offer views of the area. Unpaved Round Top Road (3N90) is about a mile west of Forest Road 3N17H, and leads a mile south to Granite Mountain and 3 miles south to Round Top. Round Top Camp, a little tent camp, is closed.

Forest Road 5N04 and the Littlerock Creek area are closed from north of Sulphur Springs to south of the Littlerock Reservoir, for the protection of endangered species. This includes two small tent camps, Little Cedars Camp and Little Sycamore Camp.

For more on the area, see Chilao Campground in this book. Supplies and gasoline are available in La Cañada, before driving more than 30 miles through the mountains to the camps. For required group reservations and other information, write or phone the Little Tujunga Work Center of the Angeles National Forest.

SITES, FEES, FACILITIES, TIME LIMITS Mount Pacifico Camp has seven nonreservable, unnumbered tent sites. A parked vehicle requires an Adventure Pass. Campsites and the loop road are dirt. There are no spurs; parking is on or near the sites. Each site has a picnic table and a metal fire ring (with grill). The camp has vault toilets, a trash bin, and an information board (no water).

Sulphur Springs Group Camp has one group site for tents and RVs. It accommodates 80 people for $100 per night. This site has picnic tables, pedestal barbecues, two metal fire rings (without grills), a concrete and rock fire ring (without grill), a water spigot, and trash cans. Vault toilets are on the north side of the stream near the information board. Parking is on the site, which is dirt. Each of the three small sites has at least one picnic table and a metal fire ring (with grill). An RV dump station is on Highway 2, about 10 miles south of camp, near Charlton Flat Picnic Area.

The Pacific Crest Trail's blacktop parking lot, west of Highway 2, has vault toilets. The parking area at Sulphur Springs gate is dirt. A vehicle parked for day use requires an Adventure Pass.

Mount Pacifico and Sulphur Springs Camps are usually open from mid-May to mid-November. The camping limit is 14 days.

Caution: Mount Pacifico Camp is reached by narrow, winding dirt roads that are rough, rutty, and rocky in places. Some places have falling rock from slides. Roads hug the edges of cliffs with steep dropoffs. At times, the roads are crossed by runoffs. On the access road, a sign says that high-clearance vehicles are advised. The camp road is bouldery and bumpy, with rocky protrusions and holes. Trailers and motorhomes are not recommended. Another sign says that this is bear country. The access road to Sulphur Springs Group Camp is partly dirt and is crossed by a stream.

DIRECTIONS From I-210 in La Cañada, take State Highway 2 (Angeles Crest Highway) north about 28 miles to Forest Road 3N17 (Santa Clara Divide Road). Turn left (west) and go 4 miles to a fork. Bear left (west) on Forest Road 3N17 as it becomes dirt. Go about 3 miles to unpaved Forest Road 3N17H. Turn right (north) and go 1.5 miles to Mount Pacifico Campground at the end of the road. Signs in the area refer to the campground as *Pacifico*, but the U.S. Forest Service's brochures, maps, and website refer to the campground as *Mount Pacifico*.

Back at the fork where Forest Road 3N17 becomes a dirt road, bear right (north) on Forest Road 5N04. Go about a mile (the road bends east). At the next fork, there is a day-use dirt parking area. Forest Road 5N04 to the left (north) to Littlerock Creek has a gate that is closed indefinitely. The access road to the right (east) also has a gate, and if this gate is open, go less than a mile to the road's end and the group campsite at Sulphur Springs Group Camp.

Buckhorn Campground

GENERAL SETTING (LOCATION, FEATURES, SUPPLIES, INFORMATION) The scenic Buckhorn Flat area near Kratka Ridge, about halfway between La Cañada and Wrightwood, is the location of this primitive national forest camp. The camp's access road drops down from the highway into the wide bottom of a steep-sided canyon where there are boulder formations, pines, and cedars; many sites are shaded. Some sites sit at the bottom; others sit a little higher in the canyon. A stream flows through the canyon, and fishing is permitted. The access road is a one-way road, and the camp is exited about half a mile east of the point where it is entered. The campfire center has benches and a rock fire pit.

Though the campground is not open during winter, skiing is a popular day-use recreational activity in the area at that time. Two popular local ski spots are Mount Waterman Ski Lifts, west of camp, and Snow Crest at Kratka Ridge, east of camp.

At Cloudburst Summit, west of camp, there is a small dirt trailhead parking area for the Pacific Crest and Silver Moccasin Trails, near Mount Waterman Ski Lifts. From Buckhorn Campground, Burkhart Trail (10W02) leads north less than 2 miles to Cooper Canyon Falls and to the Pacific Crest Trail, on which is located Cooper Canyon Trail Camp, a few miles west.

Two small picnic areas are located in the Kratka Ridge area. Vista Picnic Area, about 2 miles east of camp, sits on the side of a hill with a view at the top. The hill is steep and not suitable for wheelchairs. Eagles Roost Picnic Area, about 3 miles east of camp, is fairly level. It is set on a little pine flat at the foot of a hill next to the highway, and has a limited view through the trees of the hills to the south and the San Gabriel Wilderness. The parking lot also serves as a trailhead parking lot for the Pacific Crest Trail.

Jarvi Memorial Vista, located about 5 miles east of camp, overlooks the San Gabriel Wilderness to the south, from an attractive flagstone platform with a rail fence. A memorial plaque honors

Simeri Jarvi, a forest supervisor. Nearby, Sierra Alta Nature Trail leads west. East of Jarvi Memorial Vista is Islip Saddle Trailhead, from which the Pacific Crest Trail leads south a few miles to Little Jimmy Trail Camp and to Mount Islip.

At times, a camp host is present. Supplies and gasoline are available in La Cañada. For more information, contact the Los Angeles River Ranger District Office of the Angeles National Forest.

SITES, FEES, FACILITIES, TIME LIMITS There are 38 nonreservable, numbered campsites for tents or RVs (no hookups). The nightly fee is $12 per site. The camp road and parking spurs are blacktop; sites are dirt. The maximum RV length is about 22 feet.

Each campsite has a picnic table, a pedestal barbecue, and a metal fire ring (without grill). The camp has water spigots, vault toilets, dumpsters, and a pay phone. Signs say to please conserve water. An RV dump station is located on State Highway 2, about 12 miles southwest of camp, and is near Charlton Flat Picnic Area.

Vista and Eagles Roost Picnic Areas have picnic tables, vault toilets, and benches. Eagles Roost has a few pedestal barbecues, a trash bin, and a large blacktop parking lot. At Vista Picnic Area, park is limited to the blacktop parking strip along the highway. Jarvi Memorial Vista has a blacktop parking lot and a vault toilet.

Cooper Canyon Trail Camp has eight sites. Little Jimmy Trail Camp has 16 sites. Both camps have picnic tables, grills, vault toilets, and hitching rails. A vehicle parked at a picnic area, a trail camp's trailhead, or at Jarvi Vista requires an Adventure Pass.

Buckhorn Campground is usually open from May to October. The camping limit is 14 days. *Caution:* The camp's access road is narrow, inclined, and crossed by streams and runoffs.

DIRECTIONS From I-210 in La Cañada, take State Highway 2 (Angeles Crest Highway) north about 33 miles (the highway bends east). The camp's access road is on the highway's left (north) side.

Coldbrook Campground

GENERAL SETTING (LOCATION, FEATURES, SUPPLIES, INFORMATION) Rocky, steep-walled San Gabriel Canyon, north of Azusa, is the location of this primitive camp (elevation: 3350 feet). Its name stems from an old resort of the early 1900s, later used as a military base before it was destroyed by a flood. The camp sits on a terrace halfway up the hillside that forms the west wall of the canyon. Oaks and pines shade several sites, and a streamlike runoff flows seasonally through camp. The access road is a one-way road; the camp is exited about half a mile north of the point where it is entered. During summer, a camp host is present.

West Fork Trail wanders along the West Fork of the San Gabriel River, west of San Gabriel Canyon. Hiking, horseback riding, and bicycling are permitted on the trail, but no motor vehicles. The trail borders the San Gabriel Wilderness to the north; a wilderness permit is not required for entry here. Glenn Trail Camp, a hike-in camp, is near this trail, more than 10 miles west of Highway 39. This camp is wheelchair accessible, and the trail is open by permit to vehicles carrying persons with wheelchairs. The West Fork of the river, stocked with trout, is a "catch and release" fishing area only. Fishing platforms and ramps are provided.

The fairly small Oaks Picnic Area is located on East Fork Road, about 5 miles east of State Highway 39. East of the picnic area is East Fork Trailhead, an entry point into the Sheep Mountain Wilderness. A wilderness permit is required at this entry point.

San Gabriel Canyon OHV Area is located in the floodplain north of the San Gabriel Reservoir, near the junction of Highway 39 and East Fork Road. For day-use fees, see below. Near the OHV area, Rincon OHV Route (2N24) goes west several miles.

Supplies and gasoline are available in Azusa. A store on East Fork Road, 3 miles east of Highway 39, has limited supplies.

San Gabriel Canyon Information Station, open weekends, is located on Highway 39, about a mile north of Sierra Madre Avenue. For more information, write or phone the San Gabriel River Ranger District Office of the Angeles National Forest.

SITES, FEES, FACILITIES, TIME LIMITS The camp has 22 nonreservable, numbered campsites for tents or RVs (no hookups). The nightly fee is $8 per site. The camp road is partly blacktop and partly dirt. Parking spurs are blacktop; some are unlevel. Campsites are dirt. The maximum RV length is about 22 feet.

Each campsite has a picnic table and a metal fire ring (with grill). The camp has water spigots, vault toilets, and a dumpster.

The day-use parking fee at Coldbrook Campground is $4 per vehicle. A Los Angeles County Parking Permit ($3) is required on weekends and holidays for vehicles parked on State Highway 39 (San Gabriel Canyon Road) or East Fork Road. An Adventure Pass is accepted in place of this parking permit. Obtain permits at San Gabriel Canyon Information Station on Highway 39.

San Gabriel Canyon OHV Area has vault toilets, a pay phone, and a parking lot. Fees, weekends and holidays only, are $5 per primary vehicle and $3 per secondary vehicle (dirt bike, ATV, etc.).

Glenn Trail Camp has 10 sites, tables, grills, and vault toilets. Oaks Picnic Area has eight picnic sites, tables, grills, and vault toilets. Facility information was not verified on site. A vehicle parked at the picnic area or camp's trailhead requires an Adventure Pass.

Coldbrook Campground is usually open all year. The camping limit is 14 days. *Caution:* The access road is crossed by runoffs.

DIRECTIONS From I-210 in Azusa, take State Highway 39 north about 20 miles to Forest Road 2N02. Turn left (west); go to camp.

Crystal Lake Campground and Deer Flats Group Camp

GENERAL SETTING (LOCATION, FEATURES, SUPPLIES, INFORMATION) The Crystal Lake Recreation Area, part of the Angeles National Forest, is located near where San Gabriel Canyon Road ends, about 30 miles north of Azusa. The recreation area includes Crystal Lake Camp, Deer Flats Group Camp, Fawnskin Picnic Area, Lake Picnic Area, and Crystal Lake Visitor Center.

The camps are set on a wide flat at the end of and above the canyon. Pines, firs and oaks shade some sites. The elevation is 5800 feet at Crystal Lake Camp, and 6200 feet at Deer Flats Camp.

Crystal Lake Visitor Center, open weekends during summer, features exhibits, books, and maps. Campfire programs are given nearby at the Yerba Santa Amphitheater during summer.

Several trails wander through the Crystal Lake Recreation Area, most of them only a mile or two in length. Inquire about the trails and obtain a trail guide brochure at Crystal Lake Visitor Center. Tototngna Nature Trail, a loop of less than a mile, takes you through the Place of Stones. Near Crystal Lake Camp, Lake Trail leads west about a mile through the woods to Crystal Lake, and Cedar Canyon Trail leads east and crosses Cedar Creek. Pinyon Ridge Nature Trail is a mile loop with a view from the ridge.

Fishing is permitted in Crystal Lake, stocked seasonally with rainbow trout. The limit is five trout per day. Boating on the lake is restricted to lightweight, non-motorized small craft such as rafts.

Fawnskin Picnic Area is in a pine grove near the visitor center. The little Lake Picnic Area is near Crystal Lake, off Lake Road. For more about the area, see Coldbrook Campground in this book.

At times, a camp host is present in Crystal Lake Campground. A small store and snack bar, open limited hours, are near the visitor center. Supplies and gasoline are available in Azusa.

San Gabriel Canyon Information Station, open weekends, is on Highway 39, about a mile north of Sierra Madre Avenue. For more information, phone the concessionaire or contact the San Gabriel River Ranger District Office of the Angeles National Forest.

SITES, FEES, FACILITIES, TIME LIMITS Crystal Lake Campground has 176 numbered family campsites for tents or RVs (no hookups), divided among several loops. The nightly fee is $12 per site. Reservations are $8.65 per site. Camp roads and spurs are blacktop; sites are dirt. The maximum RV length is about 22 feet.

Each family campsite has a picnic table and a metal fire ring (with grill) or a pedestal barbecue, or both. The camp has water spigots, dumpsters, and restrooms with sinks and flush toilets.

Deer Flats Group Camp has nine group sites of different sizes. Depending on how many people each site can accommodate, nightly fees range from $40 for 20 people at one site, to $600 for 300 people at all sites combined. Reservations are required and are $8.65 per site. The maximum RV length is about 22 feet.

Group sites have picnic tables, service tables, barbecues, fire rings, water spigots, and restrooms with sinks and flush toilets.

Fawnskin and Lake Picnic Areas have picnic tables, barbecues, trash containers, and parking lots. Fawnskin has flush toilets; Lake has vault toilets. The parking fee is $5 per vehicle.

A Los Angeles County Parking Permit is required, on weekends and holidays, for vehicles parked on State Highway 39 (San Gabriel Canyon Road) or East Fork Road. An Adventure Pass is accepted in place of this parking permit. Obtain permits at San Gabriel Canyon Information Station on Highway 39.

No swimming is allowed in Crystal Lake. Deer Flats Camp, Lake Picnic Area, and their access roads were closed at the time of this writing, so facility information was not verifiable on site.

Crystal Lake Camp is usually open except during inclement weather. Deer Flats Camp is usually open from Memorial Day to the last weekend of September. The camping limit is 14 days. *Caution:* Roads are narrow, winding, and crossed by streams or runoffs.

DIRECTIONS From I-210 in Azusa, take State Highway 39 north about 27 miles. The highway bends west, then reaches Crystal Lake Road. Turn right (north) and enter the Crystal Lake Recreation Area. Go about 2 miles to Crystal Lake Camp. Follow the signs and go north about a mile farther to Deer Flats Group Camp.

LOS ANGELES COUNTY
MOUNTAIN AREA
BIG PINES AREA

1. Table Mountain Camp
2. Blue Ridge Camp
3. Guffy Camp
4. Lupine Camp
5. Cabin Flat Camp
6. Jackson Flat Grp. Camp
7. Apple Tree Camp

8. Peavine Camp
9. Mountain Oak Camp
10. Lake Camp
11. Sycamore Flats Camp
12. South Fork Camp
13. Big Rock Camp

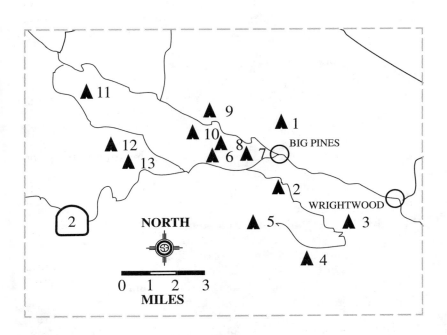

Table Mountain Campground

GENERAL SETTING (LOCATION, FEATURES, SUPPLIES, INFORMATION) Table Mountain, the home of this primitive but attractive and spacious camp in the pines, rises above the Big Pines crossroads in the Big Pines Recreation Area of the Angeles National Forest. The mountain is truly flat on top, earning its name.

Visitors to the Big Pines area have the unique experience of being in the transition zone between two natural regions of great contrast. The San Gabriel Mountains, which rise to the south, have freezing winter weather and snow blizzards. The Mojave Desert, which stretches to the north, has blistering summer weather with temperatures that soar beyond 110° at times. Mountain pines and desert Joshua trees can be seen together near Pinyon Ridge, a few miles away. The campground is situated at a good point for exploring either region. It is a mile from State Highway 2, the Angeles Crest Highway, which leads west into the San Gabriel Mountains, and leads east to highways that traverse the Mojave Desert.

From Big Pines, Table Mountain Road gradually inclines about a mile up the mountain, passing through a small residential village of cabins. The campground is located near the end of the road, close to the top, and Ski Sunrise is a short distance farther at the end of the road, right on top. The camp sits below Table Mountain Road, with it campsites on the side of the not-too-steep mountain. The elevation is 7200 feet. Many sites are shaded by pines. Some campsites have partial views through the pines of the desert to the north, and of the pine-covered mountains to the south.

The campground is not open in the winter, but skiers have their choice of two local ski areas for day use—nearby Ski Sunrise, already mentioned, and Mountain High Ski Area on Highway 2, less than a mile southeast of Big Pines. Each of these ski areas has a ski lift, a ski school, equipment rentals, a cafeteria, and a snack bar. Ski Sunrise is open from December through April, and Mountain High is open from Thanksgiving to Easter.

The small Table Mountain Picnic Area on Table Mountain Road, beyond camp, is provided for daytime picnics in the pines. Table Mountain Nature Trail (08W35) is a short, half-mile loop that is suitable for families with little children. It starts at the camp's access road just north of Table Mountain Road.

The Big Pines Recreation Area includes this campground, several nearby campgrounds, and several day-use picnic areas. Big

Pines Information Station, near the intersection of State Highway 2 and County Highway N-4, is open seasonally on weekends, and has brochures, books, maps, and campfire permits.

Supplies and gasoline are available in Wrightwood. For additional information, phone the concessionaire, or write or phone the Mojave Work Center of the Angeles National Forest.

SITES, FEES, FACILITIES, TIME LIMITS The campground has 115 nonreservable, numbered family campsites for tents or RVs (no hookups). The nightly fee is $13 per site. The camp has a blacktop road and parking spurs; some spurs are not level. The camp has dirt campsites, some with patches of grass. The maximum RV length is about 32 feet. At times, a camp host is present.

Each family campsite has a picnic table and a metal fire ring (with grill) or a triangular fire pit (with grill). Some sites also have a pedestal barbecue or a food locker. The camp has vault toilets, a dumpster, and an information board. Piped water is available during summer.

The group site has picnic tables, pedestal barbecues, a fire ring, a food locker, and a small parking lot. The nightly fee is $52.

Table Mountain Picnic Area has a few picnic tables, a trash bin, and vault toilets. A parked vehicle requires an Adventure Pass.

Outside the nearby Ski Sunrise building are soft drink machines, dumpsters, and a large blacktop parking lot for day use.

Table Mountain Campground is usually open from May to November. The camping limit is 14 days.

DIRECTIONS From Wrightwood, take State Highway 2 west about 4 miles to Table Mountain Road in Big Pines. Turn right (north) and go about a mile to the camp entrance on the left.

Blue Ridge and Guffy Campgrounds

GENERAL SETTING (LOCATION, FEATURES, SUPPLIES, INFORMATION) The Blue Ridge affords a fine view in places of the desert's Victor Valley to the north and of Mount Baldy and the Sheep Mountain Wilderness to the south. These primitive national forest camps are located near the top of the ridge, west of Wrightwood, and are a few miles apart. The elevation is 8000 feet at Blue Ridge Campground, and 8300 feet at Guffy Campground.

Blue Ridge Camp is set below the Blue Ridge on a somewhat rolling flat that drops off to the west, and Blue Ridge Trail is nearby (see below). Guffy Camp, situated near the top of the ridge, has a good view southwest of a neighboring wide canyon and hills, and a limited view north through the trees of the desert. Both camps are shaded by pines; some pines are fire-damaged in and near Guffy Camp. The forest road rises higher toward the top of the ridge between Blue Ridge Camp and Guffy Camp, and at points is on top of the ridge with views on both sides.

At Blue Ridge Summit, East Blue Ridge Road meets State Highway 2 (Angeles Crest Highway). From the trailhead parking lot at this crossroad, Lightning Ridge Nature Trail goes north, and the Pacific Crest Trail, a national scenic trail, goes west and southeast; it parallels the Blue Ridge in places. From Blue Ridge Campground, the Pacific Crest Trail leads east to Acorn Trail (07W01), which in turn leads east about 2 miles to the end of Acorn Drive in Wrightwood.

Blue Ridge Trail (08W28) stretches about 2 miles from the Pacific Crest Trail at Blue Ridge Camp to Big Pines Visitor Center, at the crossroads in Big Pines. Mine Gulch Trail (08W03), 4.5 miles in length, goes southeast from Vincent Gap Trailhead through the Sheep Mountain Wilderness. Vincent Gap Trailhead is on Highway 2, about 3 miles west of East Blue Ridge Road.

Supplies and gasoline are available in Wrightwood. For additional information, write or phone the Mojave Work Center of the Angeles National Forest.

SITES, FEES, FACILITIES, TIME LIMITS Blue Ridge Camp has eight campsites for tents or RVs. Guffy Camp has six campsites for tents or small RVs. All sites are nonreservable. A parked vehicle requires an Adventure Pass. Blue Ridge Camp's road is potholed blacktop; Guffy's is dirt. Both camps' sites and spurs are dirt; spurs are small and unlevel. The maximum RV length is about 24 feet at Blue Ridge Camp, and about 15 feet at Guffy Camp.

At both camps, each site has a table and a metal fire ring (with grill). The camps have vault toilets but no water or hookups.

At the Pacific Crest Trail on Highway 2, there is a blacktop parking lot, a vault toilet, an information board, and a trash bin.

Blue Ridge and Guffy Camps are usually open from June to October, or until the first snowfall. The camping limit is 14 days. *Caution:* The road to the camps is narrow, winding, and rocky in places due to slides. It hugs the edge of the cliff with steep drops below. It is blacktop with potholes as far as Blue Ridge Camp, then is rough dirt on the way to Guffy Camp. Guffy's dirt access road is uphill. Trailers and motorhomes are not recommended.

DIRECTIONS From Wrightwood, take State Highway 2 west about 6 miles to East Blue Ridge Road (Forest Road 3N06) at Blue Ridge Summit. Turn left (south) and go about 3 miles to Forest Road 3N06A. Turn right (west) and enter Blue Ridge Camp. On unpaved East Blue Ridge Road, go about 3 miles farther to unpaved Forest Road 3N06B. Turn left (east) and enter Guffy Camp.

Lupine and Cabin Flat Campgrounds

GENERAL SETTING (LOCATION, FEATURES, SUPPLIES, INFORMATION) Lupine Campground is named for the blue-violet flowers which make their appearance early in the spring. The Antelope Valley is widely known for its spring wildflowers. Though these two camps are not yet open at that time, other camps such as Sycamore Flats Camp and Big Rock Camp are open.

These primitive national forest camps are located in the Prairie Fork area, west of Wrightwood and the Blue Ridge. They are walk-in camps. Prairie Fork (a creek) flows by Cabin Flat Camp and near Lupine Camp. The elevation is 6500 feet at Lupine Camp, and 5300 feet at Cabin Flat Camp.

Upper Fish Fork Trail (08W10) leads from Lupine Campground southwest 4.5 miles into the Sheep Mountain Wilderness. Trail camps in the Fish Fork area have been removed. For more about the area, see Blue Ridge Campground in this book.

Supplies and gasoline are available in Wrightwood. For additional information, write or phone the Mojave Work Center of the Angeles National Forest.

SITES, FEES, FACILITIES, TIME LIMITS Lupine Camp has 11 tent sites, and Cabin Flat Camp has 12 tent sites. All sites are nonreservable. At Lupine Camp, spurs are small; the maximum RV length is about 16 feet. At Cabin Flat, park and walk in only. A parked vehicle requires an Adventure Pass.

At both camps, each site has a picnic table and a metal fire ring (with grill). Each camp has vault toilets but no water.

Both campgrounds and Forest Road 3N39 were closed at the time of this writing, so facility information was not verifiable on site. The camps are usually open from June to October, or until the first snowfall. The camping limit is 14 days. *Caution:* The rough dirt roads are recommended for four-wheel-drive vehicles.

DIRECTIONS From Wrightwood, take State Highway 2 west about 6 miles to East Blue Ridge Road (Forest Road 3N06) at Blue

Ridge Summit. Turn left (south), and go about 3 miles, passing Blue Ridge Camp, at which the pavement ends. Continue about 3 miles to Forest Road 3N39 (dirt). Turn right (west) and go about 3 miles to Lupine Camp. Go about 3 miles farther to the end of the road and Cabin Flat Camp. A sign gives the approximate mileage.

Jackson Flat Group Camp

GENERAL SETTING (LOCATION, FEATURES, SUPPLIES, INFORMATION) This national forest group camp is nicely set among pines and firs in the Big Pines Recreation Area. Only tent camping is permitted. An observation deck is a special feature. After going through the gated entrance to Grassy Hollow Visitor Center and Grassy Hollow Picnic Area, the group camp is about a mile farther inside. The elevation at camp is 7400 feet.

Jackson Flat Interpretive Trail (08W04) and Jackson Flat Geological Trail are nature trails accessed at the campground. These half-mile loops offer pleasant hikes that are not strenuous.

Grassy Hollow Picnic Area was formerly Grassy Hollow Campground, and picnicking is permitted but not camping. Fragrant pines shade picnic sites on gentle slopes above the access road. To the south, through the trees, are views of the mountains. Grassy Hollow Visitor Center, open on weekends when the weather permits, is a modern cabin-style building, level with the highway.

A trailhead with parking for the Pacific Crest Trail is on State Highway 2, about half a mile east of Grassy Hollow.

Supplies and gasoline are available in Wrightwood. For further information, write or phone the Mojave Work Center of the Angeles National Forest.

SITES, FEES, FACILITIES, TIME LIMITS There are five group tent sites. Sites 1, 2, and 3 accommodate 40 persons each, for $90 per site, per night; site 2 is the largest. Sites 4 and 5 accommodate 30 persons each, for $75 per site, per night. Sites 3, 4, and 5 are close together for large groups. All sites accommodate a combined total of 180 people. Camping fees are payable in advance.

A nonrefundable reservation fee of $20, payable in advance, is required. Group sites have picnic tables and large barbecues. The camp has two fire rings, piped water, and flush toilets.

Grassy Hollow Picnic Area has picnic tables, pedestal barbecues, and vault toilets. The visitor center has benches, flush toilets, and information boards. A blacktop parking lot and dumpster serve both areas. A parked vehicle requires an Adventure Pass.

The camp and its access road were closed at the time of this writing, so facility information was not verifiable on site. The camp is usually open from May to October. The camping limit is 14 days.

DIRECTIONS From Wrightwood, take State Highway 2 west 6.5 miles to Forest Road 3N26C. Turn right (north) and pass Grassy Hollow Visitor Center and Picnic Area. Go to the camp's gated access road, and when given permission to enter, go about a mile farther to the group camp.

Apple Tree and Peavine Campgrounds

GENERAL SETTING (LOCATION, FEATURES, SUPPLIES, INFORMATION) Somewhat steep slopes on pine-shaded hills by the highway are the settings of these primitive little tent camps in the Angeles National Forest. The campgrounds are located close to each other, nearly midway between Wrightwood and Valyermo. At Apple Tree, some sites go farther up the hill than at Peavine, and a dense growth of pines can be seen toward the top of the hill. Campsites at both camps have a limited view across the highway.

Fishing is permitted nearby at Jackson Lake, northwest of Lake Campground. For descriptions of Mountain High Ski Area and Ski Sunrise, see Table Mountain Campground in this book.

Arch Picnic Area sits on the side of a fairly steep hill that rises above then drops below the highway, and has a view of the pines. This primitive picnic area is located on Highway N-4, about 2 miles southeast of Apple Tree Campground. The elevation is 6800 feet. The steepness of the terrain is not suitable for wheelchairs.

The elevation at each camp is 6000 feet. Supplies and gasoline are available in Wrightwood. For additional information, write or phone the Mojave Work Center of the Angeles National Forest.

SITES, FEES, FACILITIES, TIME LIMITS Apple Tree Camp has eight tent sites, and Peavine Camp has four tent sites. All sites are nonreservable. A parked vehicle requires an Adventure Pass. Both camps have a small dirt parking area from which to walk to the campsites, which are also dirt.

At both camps, each campsite has a picnic table and a metal fire ring (with grill). Each camp has vault toilets, a trash bin, and an information board. Piped water is available during summer.

Arch Picnic Area has picnic tables and vault toilets (no grills). A parked vehicle requires an Adventure Pass. Walk a few yards from the dirt parking area at the entrance.

Apple Tree Campground and Peavine Campground are usually open from May to November. The camping limit is 14 days.

DIRECTIONS From Wrightwood, take State Highway 2 west about 4 miles to Big Pines Road (County Highway N-4) in Big Pines. Turn right (northwest) and go about 2 miles to Apple Tree Campground, then go about half a mile to Peavine Campground. Both camps are on the left (south) side of the highway.

Mountain Oak and Lake Campgrounds

GENERAL SETTING (LOCATION, FEATURES, SUPPLIES, INFORMATION) In a small narrow valley in the lower mountains near Big Pines lies attractive little Jackson Lake. Mountain Oak and Lake Campgrounds respectively sit on the northern and southern hills that form this valley and are diagonally opposite each other. The camps are located about halfway between Wrightwood and Valyermo, at an elevation of 6100 feet. The lake separates Jackson Lake Picnic Area from the valley highway.

Mountain Oak Campground is situated in an inviting pine forest of fairly medium density. Campsites go up the side of a hill on a loop road, and are set on rolling terrain that is not too steep. Some campsites are shaded.

Lake Campground's sites go up the foot of a slope near the southeast end of Jackson Lake. Fishing and non-motorized boating are permitted at the lake, but swimming is not recommended. Jackson Lake Picnic Area, with its pines, other shade trees, grass, and fine view of the lake, is the most scenic of the local picnic areas. The entrance is across the highway from Mountain Oak Camp. Mescal Picnic Area is across the highway from Lake Camp. A long walk on a board walkway leads to picnic sites that slope downward on the side of a hill—not an ideal place for wheelchairs. Jackson Lake Picnic Area is level.

Jackson Lake Trail (08W18) leads 2.4 miles from Jackson Lake to the Pacific Crest Trail. Devils Punchbowl County Park is near Valyermo; see Sycamore Flats Campground in this book.

Supplies and gasoline are available in Wrightwood. For additional information, phone the concessionaire or contact the Mojave Work Center of the Angeles National Forest.

SITES, FEES, FACILITIES, TIME LIMITS Both camps have nonreservable, numbered campsites for tents or small RVs (no hookups). Mountain Oak Campground has 17 sites. Lake Campground has eight sites. At both camps, the nightly fee is $12 per site. Both camps have blacktop roads and dirt sites. Mountain Oak Camp has dirt spurs; Lake Camp has blacktop spurs. Spurs are small and not level. The maximum RV length is about 18 feet.

At both campgrounds, each campsite has a picnic table and a metal fire ring (with grill). Some sites have food lockers. Mountain Oak Camp has flush toilets, and Lake Camp has vault toilets. Each camp has dumpsters and an information board. Piped water is available during summer.

Jackson Lake Picnic Area has picnic tables, pedestal barbecues, vault toilets (some with wheelchair access), a dumpster, a trash bin, and a blacktop parking lot. Vault toilets and another parking lot for fishing are on State Highway 2 at the north side of the lake. Mescal Picnic Area has picnic tables, barbecues, trash bins, and a small parking lot. A vehicle parked at any of these day-use parking lots requires an Adventure Pass.

Mountain Oak Campground and Lake Campground are usually open from May to November. The camping limit is 14 days.

DIRECTIONS From Wrightwood, take State Highway 2 west about 4 miles to Big Pines Road (County Highway N-4) in Big Pines. Turn right (northwest) and go about 3 miles to Lake Camp on the left (south) side of the highway. Continue about half a mile to Mountain Oak Camp on the right (north) side of the highway. Across the highway on the south side is Forest Road 4N49B, which leads to Jackson Lake Picnic Area and the south side of the lake.

Sycamore Flats Campground

GENERAL SETTING (LOCATION, FEATURES, SUPPLIES, INFORMATION) The Big Rock Creek area, south of the Pinyon Ridge, is the setting of this primitive national forest camp. Fishing is permitted in Big Rock Creek, across the highway from the campground. The Pinyon Ridge area, southeast of Valyermo, is a transition zone between the mountains and desert, and pines can be seen together with Joshua trees, around and near the ridge.

The camp is not far from the rural Paradise Springs community. Big Rock Creek Road follows the creek through a narrow canyon with a few cabins, then the canyon widens and the road reaches the flats and the campground. As the camp's name implies, there are scattered sycamores in the area and campground. There are pines also, and some campsites are shaded. The elevation is 4200 feet. From camp, pines can be seen on the higher mountains to the south, whereas chaparral covers the hills to the north, next to camp.

Devils Punchbowl County Park makes a good side trip. This bowl-shaped canyon in the pines is natural testimony of the effect of earthquake faults on the region's terrain. The park has a visitor center, picnic tables, hiking trails, and a nature trail. A parking fee is charged. The park is located where County Highway N-6 ends, about 8 miles southeast of Pearblossom. The highway is also called Punchbowl Road as it approaches the park.

Supplies and gasoline are available in Wrightwood. For additional information, write or phone the Mojave Work Center of the Angeles National Forest.

SITES, FEES, FACILITIES, TIME LIMITS The campground has 11 nonreservable, unnumbered campsites for tents or RVs (no hookups). The nightly fee is $8 per site. The camp's road, spurs, and sites are dirt. The maximum RV length is about 24 feet.

Each campsite has a picnic table and a metal fire ring (with grill) or a triangular metal fire pit (with grill). At times, piped water is available. The camp has vault toilets and an information board. Trash bins, and at times, portable toilets are provided for day use along Big Rock Creek Road.

Sycamore Flats Campground is closed during winter snows, but is usually open otherwise. The camping limit is 14 days.

DIRECTIONS From Wrightwood, take State Highway 2 west about 4 miles to Big Pines Road (County Highway N-4) in Big Pines. Turn right (northwest) and go about 12 miles to Big Rock Creek Road (Forest Road 4N11.1) in Valyermo. Turn left (south) and after about a mile, the road bends southeast. Go about a mile farther to the campground on the left (north) side of the road.

South Fork and Big Rock Campgrounds

GENERAL SETTING (LOCATION, FEATURES, SUPPLIES, INFORMATION) As with Sycamore Flats, these primitive camps lie within the Big Rock Creek area, southeast of Valyermo. Pine trees beautify the mountains at the higher elevations, and can be seen from the area's roads and trails. Big Rock Camp sits next to Big Rock Creek, and South Fork Camp sits by South Fork, a fork of Big Rock Creek, and is near South Fork Trail (see below). Fishing is permitted at both locations.

South Fork Campground occupies a somewhat rolling flat at a wide place in South Fork Canyon. Big Rock Creek's South Fork flows along the west side of camp. A few short pines and scrub trees provide limited shade, otherwise the spot is fairly open. Bushes afford a degree of privacy between some campsites.

South Fork Campground is accessible to several lengthy hiking trails. Manzanita Trail (09W07) leads southeast from its trailhead, just outside the camp's entrance. Across the road from the trailhead is a small dirt parking area for day use. South Fork Trail (09W02) goes southwest from camp about 6 miles to Islip Saddle and the Angeles Crest Highway (Highway 2), from where other trails can be accessed. Devils Punchbowl Trail (10W09) leads northwest from camp several miles to Devils Punchbowl County Park, mentioned in the write-up on Sycamore Flats Camp in this book.

Big Rock Campground, set at the side of a canyon, is separated from the main road (Forest Road 4N11.2) by Big Rock Creek. Most campsites sit on the gently inclined foot of the otherwise steep canyon wall, and are well shaded by pines and tall oaks. These sites have a view across the creek of the chaparral-clad south wall of the canyon and of the creek and the brush-filled creekbed. The main road continues southeast about 2 miles to the Angeles Crest Highway (Highway 2), but is rocky and narrow, and is intended for four-wheel-drive vehicles.

The elevation is 4500 feet at these camps, located about 4 miles apart. Supplies and gasoline are available in Wrightwood. For further information, write or phone the Mojave Work Center of the Angeles National Forest.

SITES, FEES, FACILITIES, TIME LIMITS Both campgrounds have nonreservable, unnumbered campsites (no hookups). Some sites are for tents, and some sites are for tents or small RVs. South Fork Camp has 21 sites. Big Rock Camp has eight sites. A parked vehicle requires an Adventure Pass. At both camps, some sites have small, unlevel parking spurs. At other sites that do not have spurs, parking is on the sites. Camp roads, sites, and spurs are dirt. The maximum RV length is about 18 feet.

At both campgrounds, each campsite has a picnic table. At South Fork Camp, each site has metal fire ring (with grill). At Big Rock Camp some sites have a metal fire ring (with grill), or a triangular metal fire pit (with grill), or a pedestal barbecue. Both camps have vault toilets but no water. South Fork Camp has a dumpster and trash bins. Trash bins, and at times, portable toilets are provided for day use along Big Rock Creek Road.

South Fork Camp and Big Rock Camp are usually open from May to November. The camping limit is 14 days. *Caution:* The dirt roads leading to the camps are rough in places, crossed by sizable creeks and streams, and are not recommended for trailers or motorhomes. The dirt roads to Big Rock Camp are narrow and rocky.

DIRECTIONS Use directions for Sycamore Flats Campground, but stay on Big Rock Creek Road (Forest Road 4N11.1) and go about half a mile farther to the road with the sign that says SOUTH FORK CAMP 1 MILE. Turn right (south) and go about a mile to South Fork Camp at the road's end. This road's route number sign was missing, as of this writing; the road had been Forest Road 4N11A.

Continue southeast on Big Rock Creek Road, and after about 3 miles, the pavement ends. Continue on the rocky dirt road as it becomes Forest Road 4N11.2 and go a short distance to Big Rock Camp's access road. Turn right, cross the creek, and go a short distance to the campground at the end of the access road.

Near Big Pines

Orange County

Once famed for the fruit which gave the county its name, Orange county long ago outgrew its orange growing image and now ranks second only to San Francisco County in population density. Nevertheless, it still has its beautiful harbor at Newport, a beautiful ocean shoreline with fine beaches, rolling hills, and, of course, Knott's Berry Farm and Disneyland. However, nestled among its hills and along its shore are nine public campgrounds offering a wide variety of camping possibilities for both tent and RV campers. All are in close proximity and the camper should have no problems finding the campground which suits his fancy.

Casper Wilderness Park

ORANGE COUNTY COASTAL AREA

▲ 1. Bolsa Chica State Beach
▲ 2. Doheny State Beach
▲ 3. San Clemente State Beach

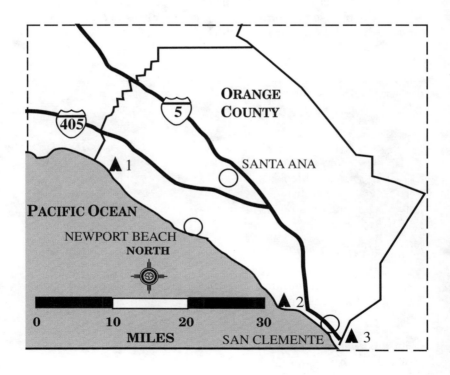

Bolsa Chica State Beach

GENERAL SETTING (LOCATION, FEATURES, SUPPLIES, INFORMATION) On clear days, Catalina Island and the Palos Verdes Peninsula can be seen from this beachfront camping area by the ocean, and across the coastal highway from the Bolsa Chica Wetlands. A paved bicycle path leads south to Huntington State Beach, where no camping is allowed. Each state beach has a sizable day-use beach with plenty of room for parking. A variety of activities awaits you, include swimming, windsurfing, and surf fishing for perch, corvina, and croaker. *Caution:* Lifeguard service is provided only during summer. Newport Beach and its famous yacht harbor is roughly 10 miles south, via State Highway 1.

Supplies and gasoline are available on State Highway 1 in Huntington Beach, about 5 miles south of Bolsa Chica State Beach. The state beach store carries food and soft drinks. For additional information, write or phone Bolsa Chica State Beach.

SITES, FEES, FACILITIES, TIME LIMITS Bolsa Chica State Beach's camping area has some RV campsites with electrical and water hookups; tents are allowed. The nightly fee is $18 per site, and reservations are recommended. The camping area's road and parking spurs are blacktop. The maximum RV length is about 40 feet. Paved ramps provide wheelchair access to the beach.

Some campsites have a picnic table and a ramada. Concrete fire rings (without grills) are located nearby on the beach. Bolsa Chica's camping area and both state beaches' day-use areas have drinking fountains, pay phones, trash cans, blacktop parking lots, and restrooms with sinks and flush toilets (some with wheelchair access). The campground has also hot (pay) showers, outdoor laundry tubs, and an RV dump station. The day-use parking fee is $3 per vehicle.

Dogs are not allowed on the beach. Bolsa Chica State Beach's camping area is usually open throughout the year. From March to November, the camping limit is seven days. From December to February, the limit is 14 days.

DIRECTIONS From I-405 in Huntington Beach, exit at Springdale Street. Go south about 3 miles to Warner Avenue. Turn right (west) and go 2.3 miles to State Highway 1 (Pacific Coast Highway). Turn left (south) and go 1.5 miles to the state beach access road. Turn right (west) and proceed to the entrance station.

Doheny State Beach

GENERAL SETTING (LOCATION, FEATURES, SUPPLIES, INFORMATION) Vast vistas of the Pacific Ocean and the coast, along with sea breezes, enhance the enjoyment of a camping stay at this nicely designed state beach at Dana Point. Some campsites are situated on the beachfront. Eucalyptus and myoprom trees beautify portions of the state beach, giving some privacy but little shade. Visitors can surf, swim, or fish for perch, corvina, and croaker. *Caution:* Lifeguard service is available only during summer.

Nearby Dana Point Harbor offers a delightful place for a stroll or a boat ride. It is an Orange County park featuring a fishing pier, two marinas, boat rentals, a boat launch ramp, and a picnic area on the shore. Windsurfing, jetskiing, and kayaking are permitted. Visitors can learn about marine life at the Ocean Institute. Mariner's Village and Dana Wharf feature shops and restaurants. World-famous Mission San Juan Capistrano is located near I-5, about 3 miles north. The Saturday morning walking tour includes the mission and San Juan Capistrano's historic downtown village.

The state beach's visitor center with aquariums, a tide pool, and a gift shop are located near the entrance. At the large picnic area near the entrance, palms and lawns lend a touch of the South Pacific. The large day-use beach is located south of camp. A volleyball area is located near the picnic area and at the day-use beach. Campfire programs are given during summer at the campfire center near site 23. At times, camp hosts reside in camp.

Crystal Cove State Park is located about 12 miles north of Doheny State Beach and 2.5 miles north of Laguna Beach. It includes an underwater park for scuba divers and trail (hike-in) campsites in El Moro Canyon, about 3 miles inland from the coast. Camping visitors must register at the ranger station, and their vehicles must be parked at the parking lot near the trailhead of El Moro Canyon Trail.

Supplies and gasoline are available in Dana Point. Limited supplies, ice, a snack bar, a pay phone, and beach equipment rentals are available at the state beach's concession store (open summer only). For more information, contact Doheny State Beach.

SITES, FEES, FACILITIES, TIME LIMITS Doheny State Beach's campground has 120 campsites for tents or RVs (no hookups). Reservations are recommended. The nightly fee is $12 per site. The camp's road and parking spurs are blacktop. Campsites are dirt and sand. The maximum RV length is about 35 feet.

Each campsite has a picnic table and a metal fire ring (with grill). The camp's restrooms have sinks and flush toilets (some with wheelchair access). Some restrooms also have hot (pay) showers. Outdoor cold showers are also available. The camp has drinking fountains, water spigots, an RV water and dump station, trash cans, recycling bins, and information boards. Pay phones are near the state beach entrance and store, and at some restrooms.

Doheny State Beach's picnic area has picnic tables, pedestal barbecues, concrete fire rings (without grills), restrooms, trash cans, recycling bins, and blacktop parking lots. Use of this picnic area is subject to reservation. The day-use beach has concrete fire rings (without grills), outdoor cold showers, toilets, trash cans, and blacktop parking lots. The day-use fee is $3 per vehicle.

Dana Point Harbor's picnic area has ramadas, picnic tables, pedestal barbecues, trash receptacles, and blacktop parking lots. Its restrooms and concrete path are wheelchair accessible. Currently there is no day-use parking fee at the harbor's picnic area.

Crystal Cove State Park's trail camp has 32 sites. The nightly fee is $7 per site, and includes four persons, two tents, and one vehicle (parked at the trailhead parking lot). No pets are allowed. The camping limit is 14 days. The trail camp has pit toilets. Water and restrooms are available at the ranger station on the coast.

Dogs are not allowed on the beach. Doheny State Beach's campground is usually open all year. From June to September, the camping limit is seven days. From October to May, the limit is 15 days.

DIRECTIONS From the interchange of I-5 and I-405 in Irvine, take I-5 south 14.5 miles to the Pacific Coast Highway exit (State Highway 1). The off-ramp takes you onto Camino Las Ramblas. Turn right (west), go about a mile, and the road merges into Pacific Coast Highway. Go about a quarter mile to Dana Point Harbor Drive. Turn left, heading toward the ocean. Go a short way to the state beach entrance, and turn left, driving parallel to the ocean.

San Clemente State Beach

GENERAL SETTING (LOCATION, FEATURES, SUPPLIES, INFORMATION) The beach city of San Clemente and the coastal hills create a sensational setting for this state beach, truly one of southern California's favorites. Eucalyptus, palm, and myoprom trees add charm and coziness to some parts of the state beach. Ramadas shade some parts of the campground and picnic area. Some campsites in the campground's hookup section are situated near the bluff. Situated along the bluff are benches from which to enjoy the view of the ocean. Hiking trails connect the campground with the beach.

During summer, campfire programs are given at the campfire center near the day-use picnic area, which sits atop the bluff and has a view of the ocean. At the ocean, surfing, swimming, and fishing for perch, corvina, and croaker are popular activities. *Caution:* Lifeguard service is provided only during summer.

Dana Point Harbor, less than 10 miles north, offers day-use boating, fishing, and picnicking; see Doheny State Beach in this book. Supplies and gasoline are available nearby in San Clemente. For more information, contact San Clemente State Beach.

SITES, FEES, FACILITIES, TIME LIMITS The campground has 72 numbered family campsites with full hookups for RVs, and 85 numbered family campsites without hookups for tents (primarily) or RVs. The nightly fee is $18 per hookup site and $12 per non-hookup site. The campground's roads and spurs are blacktop, and campsites are dirt and sand. The maximum RV length is about 30 feet at hookup sites, and about 28 feet at non-hookup sites.

Each family campsite has a picnic table and a metal fire ring (with grill). Some non-hookup sites have ramadas.

The hike and bike fee is $1 per person. The hike and bike section has picnic tables, pedestal barbecues, metal fire rings (with grills), some ramadas, and trash cans.

The group campsite accommodates 50 people and 20 vehicles, and the nightly fee is $62. The group campsite has picnic tables, fire rings, trash cans, and a restroom nearby. The maximum RV length is about 30 feet.

Reservations are required for the group campsite and are recommended for family campsites.

The campground has drinking fountains, outdoor laundry tubs, an RV dump station, trash cans, and recycling bins. At the non-hookup section, there are water spigots. A pay phone is located at the state beach entrance. Restrooms have sinks and flush toilets (some with wheelchair access). Some restrooms also have hot (pay) showers.

The state beach's picnic area has picnic tables, pedestal barbecues, ramadas, trash cans, and a blacktop parking lot. The day-use parking fee is $3 per vehicle.

Dogs are not allowed on the beach. San Clemente State Beach's campground is usually open throughout the year. From June to October, the camping limit at family sites is seven days. From November to May, the limit at family sites is 15 days. The limit at the group site is seven days, year-round.

DIRECTIONS From the interchange of I-5 and I-405 in Irvine, take I-5 south about 20 miles to Avenida Calafia in San Clemente. Exit and go toward the ocean (west) about a quarter mile. At the state beach entrance, turn left (south).

Campground section, San Clemente State Beach

ORANGE COUNTY
MOUNTAIN AREA

1. O'Neill Regional Park
2. Caspers Wilderness Park
3. Upper San Juan Campground
4. Blue Jay Campground
5. Falcon Group Camp
6. El Cariso Campground

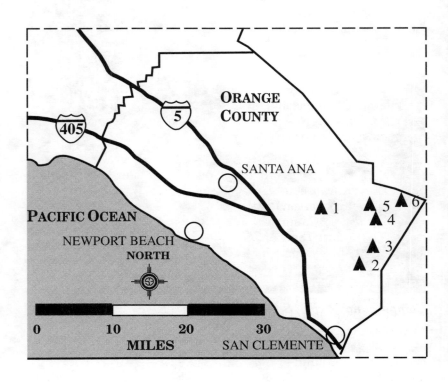

O'Neill Regional Park

GENERAL SETTING (LOCATION, FEATURES, SUPPLIES, INFORMATION) This semi-rural county park is located in Trabuco Canyon, northeast of Mission Viejo. The park is named for the O'Neill family, who formerly owned the property and donated the first parcels of land for this park to Orange County in 1948.

The park's campground sits in an appealing grassy meadow in the canyon. Oak and sycamore trees shade portions of the park and family camping area; the group camping area is mainly unshaded. The campground includes a small equestrian camping area with corrals. During the rainy season, Trabuco Creek flows through the canyon, and is separated from the campground by a berm. A low rock wall along the highway lends a country touch. At times, a camp host resides near site 15 in the family camping area.

The park features picnic areas, a playground, horseshoe pits, an arboretum, a self-guided nature trail, and a nature center, near the entrance, with a small museum focusing on local wildlife and plant life. Weekend nature hikes are led by park staff. Campfire programs are given on Saturday evenings. Trails for hiking, bicycling, and horseback riding include Pawfoot and Live Oak Trails.

Supplies and gasoline are available in Laguna Hills. A store near the park carries limited supplies. For additional information, write or phone O'Neill Regional Park.

SITES, FEES, FACILITIES, TIME LIMITS There are 85 nonreservable, numbered family campsites for tents or RVs (no hookups). There are six equestrian sites. The nightly fee per site is $10 for seniors and persons with disabilities, $12 for other persons, and $3 per horse. Camp roads are blacktop or gravel. Parking spurs are gravel or dirt. There are dirt sites, some with grass. The wheelchair site is blacktop; it has a picnic table, a pedestal barbecue, and a blacktop spur. The maximum RV length is generally about 45 feet, but a few pull-through sites accommodate even larger RVs.

Each family and equestrian campsite has one or two picnic tables and a pedestal barbecue or a fire pit (with grill), or both. Water spigots, restrooms (see below), and trash cans are provided.

Group campsites in the park accommodate 15 to 150 people. There are three adult group campsites. The nightly fee per vehicle is $10 for seniors and those with disabilities, and $12 for others. Reservations are required, and the reservation fee is $25 per group.

Each adult group site has picnic tables, a rock fire ring (without grill), a combination unit with two barbecues and a concrete serving counter, a water spigot, and trash cans. The adult group camping area has restrooms (see below) and an information board.

Two youth camping areas are for groups such as Boy Scouts and YMCA Indian Guides. The nightly fee is $5 per vehicle, $2 per passenger, and $2 for each person not staying overnight. The required reservation fee is $10 per group. These areas have picnic tables, barbecues, water spigots, and restrooms with showers.

Restrooms have sinks and flush toilets (some with wheelchair access). Restrooms near site 15 have showers. The RV dump station is located between the family and group camping areas. Pay phones are provided at the nature center and near the arboretum.

Oak Grove, Mesa, and Featherly day-use areas have picnic tables, barbecues, drinking fountains, restrooms, trash cans, and blacktop or gravel parking lots. Oak Grove also has a few picnic shelters. The day-use fee per vehicle is $4 on weekends, $2 on weekdays, and $5 to $10 on holidays.

For each dog, the nightly fee or day-use fee is $2. The campground is usually open all year. The camping limit is 15 days. *Caution:* A sign warns that this area is mountain lion country.

DIRECTIONS From I-5 in Laguna Hills, take El Toro Road (County Highway S-18) east about 7 miles to Live Oak Canyon Road (County Highway S-19). Turn right (south) and go about 3 miles. The park entrance is on the right (west) side of the road.

Caspers Wilderness Park

GENERAL SETTING (LOCATION, FEATURES, SUPPLIES, INFORMATION) A meadowlike coastal valley with oak and sycamore groves and cactus patches is the setting of this primitive but inviting county park near San Juan Creek, east of San Juan Capistrano. In the surrounding coastal hills, draped with chaparral, dwell mountain lions, bobcats, coyotes, snakes, field mice, and foxes. The elevation at this 7600-acre park ranges from 430 feet at the park entrance to 1600 feet at the highest point.

The park's name honors Ronald W. Caspers, a former chairman of the Orange County Board of Supervisors. He was responsible for the purchase of the park's land in the 1970s from the Starr family, who had owned it as a ranch for more than 30 years, and for whom the park's Starr Mesa Horse Camp is named. This camp can be used by families or groups and has corrals, hitching posts, and access to trails for horseback riding. The park has two camps with family campsites. Ortega Flats Campground sits on a grassy flat away from the hills, with some sites shaded by tall oaks. Live Oak Campground sits in a quiet glen next to a little hill. For group camping, the park has two small group sites—Owl and Quail. The park's large San Juan Meadows Group and Day-Use Area doubles as a group campsite and a picnic area, and has a playground. Old Corral Day-Use Area sits near the day-use equestrian area and the park's nature trail, a loop of less than a mile.

The park has multiple-use trails for hiking, bicycling, and horseback riding. They cover more than 25 miles and include Bell Canyon Trail, Oso Trail, East Ridge and West Ridge Trails, and San Juan Creek Trail, which parallels the creek and highway.

Weekend nature programs are given by rangers or volunteers. The park's visitor center, nature center, and office are in a small building on a little hill with a picnic table and a view of the park.

Supplies and gasoline are available in San Juan Capistrano. For additional information, phone Caspers Wilderness Park.

SITES, FEES, FACILITIES, TIME LIMITS Ortega Flats Camp has 10 sites, Live Oak Camp has 42 sites, and Starr Mesa Horse Camp has 30 sites. These are nonreservable, numbered family sites (without hookups) for tents or RVs; sites at Starr Mesa can also be used by groups. For family camping, the nightly fee per site is $10 for seniors and those with disabilities, and $12 for others. Each camp has dirt sites, some with patches of grass. Parking spurs are gravel; Starr Mesa has pull-through spurs. Roads at Live Oak Camp and Starr Mesa Horse Camp are gravel; roads at Ortega Flats Camp are dirt. The maximum RV length is about 40 feet.

At Live Oak Camp, Ortega Flats Camp, and Starr Mesa Horse Camp, each campsite has a picnic table and a pedestal barbecue; some sites at Starr Mesa also have a metal fire ring (with grill). The camps have water spigots (some with drinking fountains), portable chemical toilets, and trash cans. A restroom is located on the park's access road near Live Oak Camp. It has sinks, solar hot showers, and flush toilets (some with wheelchair access).

Six group sites at San Juan Meadows accommodate a combined total 200 people and 60 vehicles. Owl and Quail group sites together accommodate 50 people and 20 vehicles. The nightly group fee at San Juan Meadows, Owl, and Quail is $12 per vehicle; the reservation fee is $25. For youth groups such as Boy Scouts and Indian Guides, the fee is $5 per vehicle, $2 per passenger, and $2 for each person not staying overnight; the reservation fee is $10. For groups with horses at Starr Mesa, the nightly fee is $12 per site and $3 per horse; the reservation fee is $10 per site.

San Juan Meadows Group and Day-Use Area, the Owl and Quail group camping area, and Old Corral Day-Use Area have picnic tables, pedestal barbecues, water spigots (some with drinking fountains), trash cans, and restrooms with sinks and flush toilets (some with wheelchair access). The restroom at the Owl and Quail group area has solar hot showers. Roads, parking lots, and sites at these group and day-use areas are dirt.

The RV dump station is located near the park entrance. Pay phones and information boards are located near the park entrance and at the visitor center. The visitor center has a blacktop access road and a blacktop parking lot. The park's day-use fee per vehicle is $4 on weekends, $2 on weekdays, and $5 to $10 on holidays. The day-use fee is $3 per horse; no other pets are allowed.

Note: A wilderness permit is required. Caspers Regional Park's camps are usually open all year. The camping limit is 15 days.

DIRECTIONS From I-5 in San Juan Capistrano, take State Highway 74 east 7.5 miles to the park's access road and the sign that says RONALD W. CASPERS WILDERNESS PARK. Turn left (north), and go a short distance to the park entrance station.

Upper San Juan Campground

GENERAL SETTING (LOCATION, FEATURES, SUPPLIES, INFORMATION) Striking, gorge-like San Juan Canyon, in the coastal hills east of San Juan Capistrano, is the location of this primitive national forest camp. The camp sits on rolling terrain that drops a short way below the highway into the bottom of a somewhat steep bowl within the canyon. San Juan Creek flows by camp and through the canyon during the rainy season. Plenty of oak trees shade the canyon and camp. The elevation is 1800 feet.

Upper San Juan Campground lies in Riverside County, a few miles west of El Cariso Village, and is situated very close to the Orange County line. Near camp, San Juan Loop Trail offers a pleasant, 2-mile hike, and is a separate trail from the 11-mile San Juan Trail that originates at Blue Jay Campground.

Lower San Juan Picnic Area, a former campground, is restricted to day use. This small picnic area is located a quarter mile off the north side of Highway 74, about 2 miles west of Upper San Juan Camp. Like the camp, it is well shaded by oaks, and there is some grass. This picnic area sits deeper in the canyon than the campground, and is on the canyon's rocky floor next to San Juan Creek, hence the distinction between its name and the camp's name.

Supplies and gasoline are available in San Juan Capistrano. Limited supplies are available at a local store that is 0.7 mile east of camp. For further information, write or phone the Trabuco Ranger District Office of the Cleveland National Forest.

SITES, FEES, FACILITIES, TIME LIMITS The campground has 18 nonreservable, numbered campsites for tents or RVs (no hookups). The nightly fee is $15 per site. The camp has a blacktop road and dirt sites. Some campsites in small groups share blacktop parking lots. The maximum RV length is about 32 feet.

Each campsite has a picnic table and a pedestal barbecue or a metal fire ring (with grill), or both. The campground has water spigots, vault toilets, trash cans, and an information board.

Lower San Juan Picnic Area has picnic tables, pedestal barbecues, vault toilets, trash cans, an information board, and a small blacktop parking lot. A parked vehicle requires an Adventure Pass.

At times, Upper San Juan Campground and Lower San Juan Picnic Area are subject to closure for the protection of endangered species, otherwise they are usually open from May to September. The camping limit is 14 days.

DIRECTIONS From I-5 in San Juan Capistrano, take State Highway 74 east 18.5 miles. The camp entrance is on the left (north) side of the highway.

Blue Jay Campground
and Falcon Group Camp

GENERAL SETTING (LOCATION, FEATURES, SUPPLIES, INFORMATION) Blue Jay and Falcon Camps, and the removed Oriole Camp, were named for the colorful, lively birds that dwell in the hills between the Pacific Coast and the Elsinore Valley. Oriole Camp has been gone a long time, but yellow orioles and blue jays can still be observed and heard in the trees around the area.

Blue Jay Campground lies within a little basin-shaped valley, comfortably shaded by oaks and pines. Some campsites sit on the valley's gentle slopes, and some sit on the flats. Stone retaining walls at the vault toilets and at some sites add a rustic quality.

Falcon Group Camp features three group campsites next to each other on a rolling flat along the camp road. Scattered oaks and pines provide some shade, especially at Lupine group site. Falcon Trail is near the entrance.

Blue Jay Camp and Falcon Group Camp sit at elevations of 3400 and 3300 feet, respectively. These national forest camps are primitive, but are set near each other in attractive natural surroundings in the quiet Long Canyon area, north of El Cariso Village. The weather is fairly pleasant during spring and summer.

San Juan Trail extends more than 11 miles southwest from the upper trailhead at Blue Jay Camp to the lower Hot Springs Trailhead, by a vault toilet, near San Juan Fire Station on Highway 74. El Cariso Visitor Center (open limited hours) is next to El Cariso Fire Station, across Highway 74 from El Cariso Camp.

There is a view of Lake Elsinore from a turnout off North Main Divide Road, 1.5 miles north of Highway 74 and El Cariso Village.

Supplies and gasoline are available in San Juan Capistrano. Limited supplies are available at a store 2.5 miles west of Long Canyon Road. A pay phone is near El Cariso Visitor Center, a mile east of Long Canyon Road. For more information, contact the Trabuco Ranger District Office of the Cleveland National Forest.

SITES, FEES, FACILITIES, TIME LIMITS Blue Jay Camp has 55 nonreservable, numbered family campsites for tents or RVs (no hookups). The nightly fee is $15 per site. The camp has a blacktop road and dirt sites. Some sites have dirt spurs; some sites in small groups share blacktop parking lots. The maximum RV length is about 20 feet at most sites, and about 32 feet at some sites.

Most family campsites have a picnic table, a pedestal barbecue, and a metal fire ring (with grill). The campground has water spigots, vault toilets, trash cans, and information boards.

Falcon Group Camp has three group campsites. Sage group site accommodates 30 people for $50 nightly. Lupine group site accommodates 40 people for $60 nightly. Yarrow group site accommodates 70 people for $100 nightly. The reservation fee is $8.65 for each group site; larger groups may reserve more than one site. Each site is partly dirt; tables are set on blacktop. Each site has a blacktop parking lot with limited room. Lupine and Yarrow sites are mainly for tent camping. The maximum RV length is about 40 feet at Sage, about 20 feet at Lupine, and about 30 feet at Yarrow. Sage and Yarrow have limited shade; Lupine is well shaded.

Each group campsite has a few picnic tables, a serving table, a large pedestal barbecue, a metal fire ring (without grill), a water spigot, vault toilets, trash cans, and an information board.

The campgrounds are usually open from May to September. The camping limit is 14 days. *Caution:* Long Canyon Road has narrow stretches and some potholes, and is crossed by a stream.

DIRECTIONS From I-5 in San Juan Capistrano, take State Highway 74 east 21.5 miles to Long Canyon Road (Forest Road 6S05). Turn left (northwest). After 2.5 miles, the road bends north and reaches Blue Jay Campground. Falcon Group Camp is about half a mile farther. Both camps are on the road's left (west) side.

El Cariso Campground

GENERAL SETTING (LOCATION, FEATURES, SUPPLIES, INFORMATION) This national forest camp is situated in the little community of El Cariso Village, east of San Juan Capistrano. Scattered country homes dot the local hills. Unlike Upper San Juan Campground, this camp lies in a wider part of the canyon, on a rolling flat next to the highway. Instead of sloping abruptly at the steep canyon wall, the terrain inclines gradually into the hills. The elevation is 2600 feet. The campground is primitive, but is well shaded by oak trees. The area is typically southern Californian, with boulders protruding from chaparral-covered hills.

El Cariso Picnic Area, next to camp, is small and shaded by oaks. El Cariso Visitor Center (open limited hours) is next to El Cariso Fire Station, across Highway 74 from camp. El Cariso Nature Trail is a self-guided, 1.5-mile loop near El Cariso Fire Station.

The camp lies in Riverside County, close to the Orange County line. Supplies and gasoline are available in San Juan Capistrano. Limited supplies are available at two stores that are 0.5 and 3.5 miles west of camp. A pay phone and an information board are near El Cariso Visitor Center. For more information, contact the Trabuco Ranger District Office of the Cleveland National Forest.

SITES, FEES, FACILITIES, TIME LIMITS There are 24 nonreservable, numbered campsites for tents or RVs (no hookups). The nightly fee is $15 per site. The camp's road and parking spurs are blacktop; sites are dirt. The maximum RV length is about 22 feet.

Most campsites have a picnic table, a pedestal barbecue, and a metal fire ring (with grill). The camp has water spigots, vault toilets, trash cans, and an information board.

El Cariso Picnic Area has picnic tables, pedestal barbecues, a water spigot, trash cans, and a dirt parking area. Vault toilets are nearby in El Cariso Camp. The day-use fee is $5 per vehicle.

El Cariso Campground is usually open from May to September. The camping limit is 14 days.

DIRECTIONS From I-5 in San Juan Capistrano, take State Highway 74 east 22.5 miles. The camp is on the highway's north side.

Appendix 1
Los Angeles and Orange Counties
Camping Directory

For all emergency calls, dial 911.
This information is current as of Summer 2001.
Fax updates to Sunbelt Publications at (619) 258-4916.

California State Parks

Reservations (except Castaic Lake and Dockweiler) . (800) 444-7275
California Department of Parks and Recreation . . . . (916) 653-6995
   Box 942896, Sacramento, CA 94296-0001
Bolsa Chica State Beach . . . .(714) 846-3460
   18331 Enterprise Lane, Huntington Beach, CA 92648
Castaic Lake State Recreation Area—Reservations . . . .(661) 257-4050
   Box 397, Castaic, CA 91384
Crystal Cove State Park . . . .(949) 494-3539
   8471 Pacific Coast Highway, Laguna Beach, CA 92651
Dockweiler State Beach—Dockweiler RV Park . . . .(310) 322-4951
   12001 Vista del Mar, Playa del Rey, CA 90293
   Reservations . . . .(800) 950-7275
Doheny State Beach . . . .(949) 496-6172
   25300 Harbor Drive, Dana Point, CA 92629
Hungry Valley State Vehicular Recreation Area . . . .(661) 248-7007
   Box 1360, Lebec, CA 93243-1360
Huntington State Beach (Day-use) . . . .(714) 536-1454
Leo Carrillo State Beach . . . . (310) 457-1324, (818) 880-0350
   c/o Angeles District, 1925 Las Virgenes Road, Calabasas, CA 91302
   Ranger Station . . . . (805) 488-1827, (805) 488-5223
Malibu Creek State Park . . . .(818) 880-0350
   c/o Angeles District, 1925 Las Virgenes Road, Calabasas, CA 91302
   Ranger Station . . . .(818) 880-0367
Placerita Canyon State and County Park—Walker Ranch Group Camp
   19152 Placerita Canyon Road, Newhall CA 91321 . .(661) 259-7721
Saddleback Butte State Park . . . .(661) 942-0662
   c/o California State Parks, Mojave Desert Sector,
   43779 15th Street West, Lancaster, CA 93534-4754
San Clemente State Beach . . . .(949) 492-3156
   3030 Avenida del Presidente, San Clemente, CA 92672
Topanga State Park . . . .(310) 455-2465
   Closure updates (during fire danger, etc.) . . . .(805) 488-8147
   Nature walks . . . .(818) 888-6856

Orange County Parks

Caspers Wilderness Park .... (949) 728-3420
    Box 395, San Juan Capistrano, CA 92675
Dana Point Harbor (Day-use) .... (949) 661-7013
O'Neill Regional Park .... (949) 858-9365
    Box 372, Trabuco Canyon, CA 92678

U.S. Forest Service

Reservations .... (877) 444-6777
    (except Bandido, Coulter, Lightning Point, Sulphur Springs, Lake,
    Mountain Oak, Table Mountain, and Los Alamos Camps)

Angeles National Forest Headquarters .... (626) 574-1613
    701 North Santa Anita Avenue, Arcadia, CA 91006
Little Tujunga Work Center .... (818) 899-1900
    12371 Little Tujunga Canyon Road, San Fernando, CA 91342
    Reservations for Bandido, Coulter, Lightning Point,
        and Sulphur Springs Group Camps .... (818) 899-1900
Los Angeles River Ranger District Office .... (818) 790-1151
    Oak Grove Park, Flintridge, CA 91011
        Chantry Flat Information Station .... (626) 355-0712
        Chilao Visitor Center .... (626) 796-5541
Mojave Work Center .... (661) 944-2187
    Box 15, Valyermo, CA 93563
        Lake, Mountain Oak, and Table Mountain Camps—
            Concessionaire and reservations .... (800) 342-2267
        Big Pines Information Station .... (760) 249-3504
        Grassy Hollow Visitor Center .... (626) 821-6737
San Gabriel River Ranger District Office .... (626) 335-1251
    110 North Wabash Avenue, Glendora, CA 91741
        Crystal Lake Campground, Deer Flats Group Camp
            Concessionaire .... (626) 910-2848
        Crystal Lake Visitor Center .... (626) 910-1149
        San Gabriel Canyon Information Station .... (626) 969-1012
Santa Clara/Mojave Rivers Ranger District Office ... (661) 296-9710
    30800 Bouquet Canyon Road, Saugus, CA 91350
        Los Alamos Campground and Pyramid Lake—
            Concessionaire, reservations for groups ... (661) 248-6575
        Vista del Lago Visitor Center .... (661) 294-9206

Cleveland National Forest Headquarters .... (858) 673-6180
    10845 Rancho Bernardo Road #200, San Diego, CA 92127-2107
Trabuco Ranger District Office .... (909) 736-1811
    1147 East 6th Street, Corona, CA 91719
        El Cariso Visitor Information Center ...... (909) 678-3700

Critter Safety

Big Bear Discovery Center, Big Bear Ranger District. . . (909) 866-3437
   Box 290, Fawnskin, CA 92333
California Department of Fish and Game . . . . (310) 590-5132
   330 Golden Shore, Suite 50, Long Beach, CA 90802
California Department of Health Services,
   Vector-Borne Disease Section . . . . (916) 324-3738
Cooperative Extension, UCSD . . . . (800) 200-2337
   UC Cooperative Extension–AHB,
   555 Overland Avenue, Building 4, San Diego, CA 92123
Los Padres National Forest . . . . (805) 683-6711
   6144 Calle Real, Goleta, CA 93117
Trabuco Ranger District, Cleveland National Forest . . . (909) 736-1811
   1147 East 6th Street, Corona, CA 91719-1616

Appendix 2
Rules and Regulations

Check-in time is 2 P.M. and *check-out time* is 12 noon at most state parks, but at Dockweiler, check-in time is 1 P.M., and at Castaic Lake, check-out time is 10 A.M. Check-in time and check-out time is 2 P.M. at Orange County Parks and at Cleveland National Forest campgrounds. Check-in and check-out times vary from 10 A.M. to 2 P.M. at different Angeles National Forest campgrounds; phone for details.

Six to eight persons is the usual limit per family (individual) campsite. The limit per group campsite is stated under each group campsite.

Youths under 18 years of age must be accompanied by a parent or legal guardian.

Quiet time is observed from 10 P.M. to 7 A.M. at Orange County Parks, and from 10 P.M. to at least 6 A.M. at state parks and national forest campgrounds.

Generators must be turned off from 8 P.M. to 10 A.M. at state parks.

Fires are restricted to the barbecues, fire rings, fireplaces, fire pits, or other fire containers that have been installed at the campgrounds. An approved, portable metal container, off the ground, may be used at some campgrounds or camping areas that do not have fire containers; phone for details. No open ground fires are allowed. Fires are prohibited usually during fire season and periods of high fire danger.

Water is available at some camps, but where it is not, bring your own. *Caution:* Water from springs, creeks, and other natural sources is contaminated, so it must be treated and purified (by boiling, etc.), before drinking. During dry spells, water from natural sources is scarce.

Wood, flowers, plant life, wildlife, insects, rocks, artifacts, and other natural and man-made features are protected by law and may not be removed, collected, or gathered. At some Cleveland National Forest campgrounds, dead down wood may be gathered for use as firewood; phone for details. The Angeles National Forest requires a permit (fee) to gather or cut dead down wood; phone for details. Firewood is sold at a few camps.

Trash and all other refuse must be placed in the receptacles provided. Where receptacles are not provided, please carry out your trash.

Two vehicles is the usual limit per family (individual) campsite where vehicles are allowed. At many camps, the fee per family campsite includes the vehicle that tows plus the vehicle that is towed. A second vehicle, driven in, may be allowed for an extra fee of $2 to $5 at national forest camps, $4 at Orange County Parks, $5 (winter) to $6.75 (summer) at Dockweiler RV Park, and no extra fee at state-run state parks. However, at some camps the vehicle being towed counts as the second vehicle for which the extra fee (or no extra fee) is charged. These rules are somewhat complex, so phone for details. The vehicle limit per group campsite varies and is stated under most group campsites where vehicles are allowed.

Recreational vehicles (RVs), including motorhomes, trailers, pickup campers, vans, van conversions, tent trailers, etc., must be self-contained where there are no hookups or sanitary dump stations available.

The maximum RV length has been given for some family (individual) and group camping sections, but may not apply at all campsites in a section. To determine if an RV length will accommodate a trailer, use the length from the trailer's hitch to the trailer's tail end. Many campgrounds have RV lengths of 27 feet or less, and some camps can only accommodate RVs that are 15 to 20 feet long, such as pickup campers, van conversions, and small trailers. Some local campgrounds that have some campsites for longer RVs include O'Neill Regional Park (40 feet), Caspers Regional Park (45 feet and longer), state beaches and other state parks (30 to 40 feet), and a few national forest camps, including Chilao (40), Horse Flats (36), Monte Cristo (30), Table Mountain (32), and Upper San Juan (32). It is best to reserve early at reservable sites, and arrive early at nonreservable sites.

Vehicles must remain on established roads. Drivers must be licensed. Phone for regulations on motorbikes, trail bikes, and other vehicles.

Off-highway vehicles (OHVs) are also called *off-road vehicles (ORVs)*. Per state regulations, "All vehicles must either be registered street-legal vehicles or have a State of California off-highway registration (Green Sticker)." OHVs are restricted to areas and trails designated for OHV use. An Adventure Pass is not required for OHV Green Sticker use. For OHV regulations and maps of OHV areas, contact the appropriate jurisdiction.

Fishing at most campgrounds and day-use areas requires a valid California fishing license. A fee and/or a permit is required in some cases.

Hunting and firearms are not permitted in county parks and state parks. Phone for regulations and restrictions on hunting and firearms in the Angeles and Cleveland National Forests.

Dogs must be licensed, vaccinated for rabies, secured on a 6-foot leash, and confined at night in a tent or enclosed camping vehicle. Owners must clean up after their pets. In state parks and O'Neill Regional Park, dogs are not allowed on trails or near most water sources; phone for details. In national forests, dogs are not allowed near swimming areas. Regarding horses and other pets, phone for rules, regulations, and fees.

Unpaved roads should be avoided during rains or snows. They become impassable and dangerous. Phone ahead of time for road conditions.

Closures of campgrounds, roads, and trails may occur due to fires, rains, floods, snows, slides, or other unforeseen emergencies. Otherwise, the campgrounds are usually open during the periods stated in this book.

Trail and wilderness hike-in camping are beyond this book's scope. Musch Trail Camp and Millard Camp were visited. Other trail camps were not visited; information on them is from the jurisdictions and was not verified on site. Phone for information, regulations, and fire permits.

Rest areas and picnic areas may not be used for camping. Picnic areas are for daytime use only. At Caltrans rest areas, no fees are charged.

Day-use fees are given for some picnic areas and campgrounds. Adventure Passes may not be used at some Angeles and Cleveland National Forest picnic areas and campgrounds. See below, and phone for details.

 # Appendix 3
Adventure Passes

In places where camping or day-use fees are not charged in the Angeles and Cleveland National Forests, an Adventure Pass must be displayed on the parked vehicle of anyone who visits these forests for recreation. These places include campgrounds, picnic areas, trailheads, parking areas, OHV areas, and other places in the national forests where vehicles are parked. Recreation includes camping, picnicking, hiking, bicycling, horseback riding, swimming, skiing, fishing, hunting, and other activities.

A day pass costs $5. A year pass costs $30 and is valid until December 31. The fine for not displaying a pass is $100. For clarification and more information, contact one of the national forest offices. The pass may be purchased at those offices and at many sporting goods stores.

 # Appendix 4
Hazardous Critters

Usually the only creatures, other than humans, that may annoy campers are flies and mosquitos. While the probability of being struck by lightning is greater than being attacked by a mountain lion or bear, it is well to be aware that such creatures do exist in California's mountainous areas. The brochures listed below present information pertaining to these and other critters, and some precautions campers might take. The sources of these brochures are also listed below, and their phone numbers and/or addresses are given in Appendix 1.

"Bear Us in Mind," Big Bear Discovery Center, Big Bear Ranger District, San Bernardino National Forest. (Pertaining to bears.)

"Bee Alert: Africanized Honey Bee Facts," Cooperative Extension, University of California, San Diego.

"Facts about Hantavirus in California," California Department of Health Services, Vector-Borne Disease Section. (Pertaining to deermice.)

"Facts about Lyme Disease in California," California Department of Health Services, Vector-Borne Disease Section. (Pertaining to ticks.)

"Facts about Plague in California," California Department of Health Services, Vector-Borne Disease Section. (Pertaining to rodents and fleas.)

"Living With California Bears," California Department of Fish and Game

"Living With Mountain Lions," California Department of Fish and Game. *Please report any close encounters with mountain lions, any attacks, and any sightings of dead or injured mountain lions to the California Department of Fish and Game.*

"Mountain Lion Territory," Trabuco Ranger District, Cleveland National Forest.

"Watch Out for These!" Los Padres National Forest. (Pertaining to rattlesnakes and poison oak.)

Castaic Lake

Index

*Group campsite(s) available.

SUNBELT PUBLICATIONS
Adventures in the Natural and Cultural History of the Californias
Series Editor—Lowell Lindsay

SAN DIEGO SERIES:

Rise and Fall of San Diego: 150 Million Years	Abbott
More Adventures with Kids in San Diego	Botello, Paxton
Cycling San Diego, 3rd Edition	Copp, Schad
A Good Camp: Gold Mines of Julian and the Cuyamacas	Fetzer
San Diego Mountain Bike Guide	Greenstadt
San Diego Specters: Ghosts, Poltergeists, Tales	Lamb
Campgrounds of San Diego County	Tyler

SOUTHERN CALIFORNIA SERIES:

Campgrounds of Santa Barbara and Ventura Counties	Tyler
Campgrounds of Los Angeles and Orange Counties	Tyler
Portrait of Paloma: A Novel	Crosby
California's El Camino Real and Its Historic Bells	Kurillo
Orange County: A Photographic Collection	Hemphill
Mission Memoirs: Reflections on California's Past	Ruscin
Warbird Watcher's Guide	Smith

CALIFORNIA DESERT SERIES:

Anza-Borrego A to Z: People, Places, and Things	D.Lindsay
The Anza-Borrego Desert Region (Wilderness Press)	L. and D. Lindsay
Geology of the Imperial/Mexicali Valleys (SDAG 1998)	L.Lindsay ed.
Palm Springs Oasis: A Photographic Essay	Lawson
Desert Lore of Southern California, 2nd Ed.	Pepper
Peaks, Palms, and Picnics: Journeys in Coachella Valley	Pyle
Geology of Anza-Borrego: Edge of Creation	Remeika, Lindsay
California Desert Miracle: Parks and Wilderness	Wheat

BAJA CALIFORNIA SERIES:

The Other Side: Journeys in Baja California	Botello
Cave Paintings of Baja California, Rev. Ed.	Crosby
Backroad Baja: The Central Region	Higginbotham
Lost Cabos: The Way it Was (Lost Cabos Press)	Jackson
Journey with a Baja Burro	Mackintosh
Houses of Los Cabos (Amaroma)	Martinez, ed.
Baja Legends: Historic Characters, Events, Locations	Niemann
Loreto, Baja California: First Capital (Tio Press)	O'Neil
Sea of Cortez Review	Redmond

Sunbelt books celebrate the land and its people through publications in natural science, outdoor adventure, and regional interest.